Style and Story

STEPHEN J. PYNE

Style & Story

Literary Methods for Writing Nonfiction

THE UNIVERSITY OF
ARIZONA PRESS
TUCSON

The University of Arizona Press
www.uapress.arizona.edu

ISBN-13: 978-0-8165-3789-1 (paper)

Cover design by Leigh McDonald

The Wallace Stegner quotations in chapter 7 are from *Mormon Country* by Wallace Stegner. Copyright © 1942, 1970 by Wallace Stegner. Used by permission of Brandt & Hochman Literary Agents, Inc. All rights reserved.

Excerpts from "Travels of the Rock" from *Irons in the Fire* by John McPhee. Copyright © 1997 by John McPhee. Reprinted by permission of Farrar, Straus and Giroux.

Excerpts from "A Pledge to My Readers" by Michael Erard. Reproduced with permission of the author.

Excerpts from "Back from Yet Another Globetrotting Adventure, Indiana Jones Checks His Mail and Discovers That His Bid for Tenure Has Been Denied" by Andy F. Bryan. Reproduced with permission of the author.

Library of Congress Cataloging-in-Publication Data
Names: Pyne, Stephen J., 1949– author.
Title: Style and story : literary methods for writing nonfiction / Stephen J. Pyne.
Description: Tucson : The University of Arizona Press, 2018. | Includes bibliographical references and index.
Identifiers: LCCN 2017060969 | ISBN 9780816537891 (pbk. : alk. paper)
Subjects: LCSH: Authorship. | Creative nonfiction. | English language—Rhetoric. | Exposition (Rhetoric)
Classification: LCC PN145 .P957 2018 | DDC 808.02—dc23 LC record available at https://lccn.loc.gov/2017060969

Printed in the United States of America
♾ This paper meets the requirements of ANSI/NISO Z39.48-1992 (Permanence of Paper).

For Sonja
a palimpsest of thanks

Contents

Preface

In which we apply words to words, and write about writing.

This is a text about writing texts.

It builds on my earlier exploration into nonfiction writing, *Voice and Vision*. For a decade now I have taught a graduate-level course in writing; *Voice and Vision* coevolved with that experience. As I continue to teach, other topics have shouldered their way into the arena, I have found some better examples of what I wish to convey, and I am able—and happy—to let my own writing fade from the roster of samples. *Style and Story* is the outcome.

It's not clear how to designate this kind of writing. Publishers call it serious nonfiction. Readers probably call it by whatever topic the text at hand addresses; history as history, self-help as self-help, biography as biography, science as science (or popular science). I don't consider it creative nonfiction, which has spun its own cocoon of a world out of MFA filaments. Creative nonfiction has spread mostly by fiction writers colonizing the terrain of nonfiction, with the frequent outcome that argument morphs into narrative, essays into short stories, and histories into memoirs. To help quarantine the infection, one critic, Lydia Pyne, has coined the term "fact-checked nonfiction" to distinguish her work from the fact-challenged sort. Not too long ago the phrase would have seemed an oxymoron: fact-checked and nonfiction were two ways of saying the same thing. Not today.

My default term is *literary nonfiction* because I regard the project as applying literary techniques and sensibilities to nonfiction subjects, in the same way biologists might use statistics without claiming to be mathematicians. Probably a good name matters. But I don't want to burden this book or its predecessor by quarrels over nomenclature.

While this book aligns with my earlier guide, it should also stand alone.

To that end I'll repeat here what I regard as the two rules for writing nonfiction. Rule One: You can't make stuff up. That includes fusing conversational strings into new quotes, creating composite characters, or staging confrontations that might reflect known conflicts in general but did not in fact happen specifically. It means you can't rearrange timetables, tweak sources, or invent circumstances in the name of a "larger truth," aesthetic clarity, or "reading better." If you want a truth that is specially available to fiction, then write fiction. Zero tolerance here. Rule Two: You can't leave out known stuff that affects our understanding. This is a judgment call, but it is usually clear how it applies in particular cases.

The typical scenario is that sources are either too scarce or too abundant. The first tempts a bad writer to fill in the gaps; the second, to leave out what matters in the name of a sharper sketch, a brisker narrative, a more vibrant climax, or just simplicity of expression. Yet yielding to such temptations is not a mark of literary imagination but a failure of it. There are always alternatives. There are alternative word choices, alternative rhythms, alternative constructions that can do the job. Gifted writers learn how to stay within the rules. Slovenly writers cheat.

Follow these rules and you are writing nonfiction. But writing also requires that you match substance and style, so that how you say aligns with and supports what you say. Here we enter the realm of taste, and equally, those tricky circumstances where personal taste must align with collective taste. Nonfiction is a large corral that can hold lots of strays. Each group within it will have its own additional norms, mores, aesthetics, and preferred styles of presentation. What is acceptable to historians might not appeal to sociologists, what serves engineers might not pass with anthropologists, what biologists welcome philosophers might shun. There are subgroups within subgroups. What qualifies as nonfiction generically might not pass muster specifically. Writing nonfiction doesn't guarantee that you are writing philosophy as philosophers recognize it, or biology as biologists recognize it. The two rules have lots of relations and shirttail cousins that define what clan a text might claim for its own.

I began this guide as a supplement to *Voice and Vision* that might appeal to writers of history. Why? Because, by training and temperament, I'm a historian, mostly.

It began early. I read history while my friends read science fiction or sports stories. Mostly those texts reflected the style of a generation older than I. That got imprinted on my imagination. I emulated those writers when I was young, and as I matured, they provided a veiled template as I learned to write in a style more at ease with contemporary tastes. That tension remains. I started teaching writing with the notion that I would instruct historians. That didn't happen. My academic career took place outside history departments. Historians have been a minority among my students.

There are lots of explanations for why history and literature have seemingly parted ways. Certainly the postmodern turn stirred wariness over language and deep suspicion about narrative. Historians were so busy deconstructing and unpacking texts that they forgot how to build and pack them in the first place. Perhaps theses, and arguments, replaced themes as the preferred means to organize a text. There seemed less and less to unite the guild, certainly no consensus narrative, or even agreement that a narrative was possible. Instead of narrative as literary melting pot, we got a narrative salad. History was identity politics better served by personal stories, collective memoirs, and political case studies.

But while the separation may have begun among professional historians, it soon divorced historians from their publics. The public disregarded history apart from family heritage, celebrity biography, and costume dramas. Then the other disciplines weighed in. Archaeology went from a tool for history to an outright rival. Journalism filled the vacuum in public discourse and popular topics. Alarm over the contemporary crises (such as the advent of the Anthropocene) underwrote a reaction to studies of the past on the grounds that we faced a no-analogue future, that the search for a usable past matters less than the search for a usable future.

An exaggeration. But history seems to have lost both its intellectual standing and its sensibility to literature, and I think it likely those two trends are related. The vital valence between words and our understanding of the past broke. What was said overrode how it was said, forgetting that the *how* helps make the *what* possible. Not all history has to be narrative, but history without change over time is not really history so much as social science, memoir, blogging, commentary, and anecdote. The middle got lost. Long ago science settled on the working hypothesis as a compromise between theory and fact. By analogy history might look to the working narrative.

But my purpose here is not to reform professional history (not my ambition, not in my power). It's to show those interested in writing history that alternatives are possible and to illustrate some of the literary tools and strategies available. Many of the examples are drafted from historical writings because that is the field I most often work in and read. But while I began writing for historians, the text went elsewhere, and I was happy to give it its head and enjoy the ride.

My intention is that *Style and Story* will speak to nonfiction writers of all kinds. I have included samples of many nonfiction genres, not least what is usually dismissed as academic. (Bad academic writing deserves that scorn, good academic writing doesn't.) Inevitably the selections reflect my own interests and tastes.

Mindful writing makes you conscious of the options available and the consequences of choosing any one of them. That happens best by analyzing examples rather than arguing abstractly. The only way to learn to write better, however, is to write, and write, and write, and edit—self-edit—endlessly. You don't learn to play a piano by reading musical scores or to play center field by reading biographies of All-Stars. You can learn a lot about craft from reading, by studying exemplars of authors you admire and by parsing striking prose for the techniques that make it happen, and showing how to read in this way is a purpose of this guidebook. Still, while everything must be learned, not everything can be taught. You learn writing by writing.

Style and Story

1
Openings

In which we begin with beginnings and explore how to open a text in ways that engage readers and make an ending possible.

L et's start with how to start. Consider these three openings, the first to an essay, the second to a nonfiction novella, the third to a book.

In the summer of 1966 I was living in a borrowed house in Brentwood, and had a new baby. I had published one book, three years before. My husband was writing his first. Our daybook for those months shows no income at all for April, $305.06 for May, none for June, and, for July, $5.29, a dividend on our single capital asset, fifty shares of Transamerica stock left to me by my grandmother. This 1966 daybook shows laundry lists and appointments with pediatricians. It shows sixty christening presents received and sixty thank-you notes written, shows the summer sale at Saks and the attempt to retrieve a fifteen-dollar deposit from Southern Counties Gas, but it does not show the date in June on which we first met Henry Robbins.

—JOAN DIDION, "AFTER HENRY"[1]

And then he thinks he knows
The hills where his life rose. . . .

—*MATTHEW ARNOLD, "THE BURIED LIFE"*

I was young and I thought I was tough and I knew it was beautiful and I was a little bit crazy but hadn't noticed it yet. Outside the ranger station there were more mountains in all directions than I was ever to see again—oceans of mountains—and inside the station at this particular moment I was ahead in a game of cribbage with the ranger of the Elk Summit District of the Selway Forest of the United States Forest Service (USFS), which was even younger than I was and enjoyed many of the same characteristics.

—NORMAN MACLEAN, "USFS 1919: THE RANGER, THE COOK, AND A HOLE IN THE SKY"[2]

Early in the eighth century a mixed people whom history was to call the Moors crossed the Strait of Gibraltar from Africa. They went as mercenaries to break a stalemate in one of the civil wars which that people of the Iberian Peninsula have been fighting at intervals for two thousand years. but they stayed as conquerors. Within a quarter of a century they had subjugated Spain to the Pyrenees. There were no Spanish people then; the inhabitants of the Peninsula were more heterogeneous than the Moors. The eighth century was nearly over before complexities of politics, trade, religious allegiance, and philosophical speculation permitted combinations capable of military opposition. From then on the people of the Peninsula drove the Moors southward, were driven northward before resurgences of Moorish power, and paused in their war on the infidels only when domestic developments made it necessary again for them to fight one another.

The conquest, or reconquest, lasted almost exactly seven hundred years. Seven centuries of hardly intermitted war created the Spanish people and they, the most medieval people in western Europe, created the Kingdom of Spain. The seven centuries forged the Spanish soul of valor, honor, and chivalry, and tempered it in fanaticism, cruelty, and treachery. In 1492 the army of Ferdinand of Aragon and Isabella of Castile broke the last remnant of Moorish power in Spain and the conquest was complete. But there would still be a use for conquistadores: in the same year a navigator in the employ of Isabella discovered the New World.

Most Christian, most exalted, most excellent and powerful Princes, King and Queen of the Spains and of the islands of the sea: … [you] determined to send me, Christopher Columbus, to the countries of India, so that I might see what they were like, the lands and the people, and might seek out and know the nature of everything that is there. And you ordered me not to travel to the East, not to journey to the Indies by the land route that everyone had taken before me, but instead to take a route to the West, which so far as anyone knows no man had ever attempted. …[3]

— BERNARD DEVOTO, *THE COURSE OF EMPIRE*

In the folklore of writing, the opening is typically the hardest passage to write. It's hard to hit stride from a cold start, and the final version is usually the outcome of many (many) revisions. Beginnings can be full of false dawns and stutter steps. Yet for the reader the opening is often the most memorable part of a book. Or if not the most memorable, it is what encourages a reader to continue. It stays in the mind. It keeps the reader turning pages. A bad opening means the reader will never get to the conclusion, however stirring and clever.

There is no single formula for openings because they have no single purpose other than the most basic: to prod the reader onward. They convince readers to keep reading and, ideally, equip them for the task ahead. They establish authorial voice, display the text's style, pique curiosity about what will happen or where an idea will lead. For some writing the opening is an introduction, an invitation to read on; for others, it holds the core of the text, a succinct summary for which what follows is an elaboration that can be read or passed over. Or to paraphrase one of literature's most famous openings, All bad openings are alike in their failure while good openings succeed each in its own way.

The passages that open this chapter differ in how they work and how they must sit within their larger context. Didion's essay profile is about two thousand words; Maclean's novella memoir, under forty thousand; and DeVoto's quoted staggered prologue, the opening fanfare for a 647-page epic. Yet each gives us enough detail and mystery and momentum to lure us further. Each informs us what kind of literature we are reading. Each tells us what kind of voice we can expect. Each prompts us to read on.

Joan Didion entices us with a long passage of personal details, an exercise in misdirection before a final sleight of hand reveals the topic. The questions pile up: what is this about? where is it going? who, ultimately, is the subject? It all feels grounded, and tangible. We discover that it's a tribute to the recently deceased Henry Robbins, an editor with whom Didion had worked early in her career. But as it deepens it shape-shifts into an inquiry into how Didion became a writer, and what that means for anyone aspiring to write. The profile is about the lived life of a writer, about how one might become that person, which makes it an authorial coming-of-age story. Writing is often a subject for writers. But it's rare to have it so richly refracted through someone else.

Norman Maclean's novella is also a writer's coming-of-age story, though it takes place on a U.S. Forest Service trail crew in the Bitterroot Mountains in Montana when the author was seventeen years old. It's about words—literary words, words becoming literary, prose edging into the rhythms of poetry—becoming absorbed into life until the words are the life. So it opens with an epigraph, an old literary device, in this case a poem fragment whose imagery will become concrete in the telling of Maclean's summer. It seeks thematically to establish a time in his life. The style echoes that purpose, with opening run-on sentences that seem awkward, because the author, at that time, was still struggling to find the words and discipline them into meaning. That would come through the living and the thinking about how to express the life that did so much to make him who he became.

Bernard DeVoto's epic knows its ending: the crossing by Lewis and Clark that first announced the continental ambitions of the United States. But where to begin? Begin with several quotations, epigraphs (not listed above), that establish the poetry and politics of the purpose. One from a poet, one from a historian, one from the politician who held the then fractious less-than-united states together during the Civil War. Then describe the society that will dispatch the first discovers and conquerors of the New World; this will ground the narrative in historical continuities. Then quote, in italics, the first discoverer, Christopher Columbus, about what he understands his mission to be. The story that unfolds will be as much about dreams and mirages as looting and hard-on-the-ground exploration. The narrative braids several themes, and it is necessary to introduce DeVoto's voice as well as his vision. Epics that are also national creation stories can easily lose footing in inflated diction and tone, but DeVoto keeps the grandeur with his structural design, not the swelling of his sentences. Writing in the aftermath of World War II, DeVoto wants to explain to the world how the United States has fit into the past on the world stage and how that past made it what it is.

So there are lots of openings possible, some just one-liners, others complicated introductions ultimately judged by how well they serve the larger text. Yet a rude taxonomy of openings is possible. Genres differ in style, voice invites some openers and discourages others, scale allows (or disallows) among possibilities.

The major chasm is between journalism and other metastyles such as narrative history and scholarship. In journalism the lead is just that: it must open. Often the opening contains its own closing. It may simply be a punch line, a one-liner joke to get attention that does nothing further for the full text. By contrast, where arguments or narratives are involved, the opening must advance inevitably, step by step, evidence upon evidence, event after event, to a conclusion different from what began the text. Opening and closing are anchor points that hold the span of prose between them. The opening is separate from but must lead to the ending. The theme, style, and expectations of the start determine the character of the end. They share an unrendable unity. Change one part, and you change the other.

Consider three varieties of openings. One is the hook or grabber. Its purpose is to lead (yank?) the reader inside. Done well it brings readers willingly into the text before they know the door has closed behind them. Done poorly it acts as no more than the obligatory icebreaker joke of a toastmaster or, cynically, as an exercise in bait and switch. A second variant is the thesis statement of an argument. It poses the question or puzzle that the text will try to resolve. The third is the prologue to a narrative. It announces the plot—opens the action, introduces the agents, establishes the authorial point of view, and speaks in the voice that will carry the tale.

Opening as Hook

Every reader will have some favorites. Here are some of mine, all of which in some form I have adapted. Note that the selected texts do more than illustrate an opening gambit: they all hold interest as examples of voice, tempo, diction, audience identification, and good writing generally.

Anthony Lane, "Big Guy"

How's this for a snappy, one-line grabber, the opening to a review of the latest *Godzilla* movie.

Wrinkled and crinkled, huge in Japan, heroically reluctant to give up, and forever touring the world on a mission to make us scream, Godzilla is the Mick Jagger of giant amphibians.[4]

We get two for one. Lane manages to equate Godzilla with the world of endlessly touring celebrity oldsters, while equating Jagger with a camp figure of horror movies.

George Orwell, "Marrakech," "Shooting an Elephant," "A Hanging"

Orwell is a master of openings. His plain style is so direct that the text seems to open in medias res. It appears to simply begin. In fact, he does write introductions but they don't call attention to themselves as such. They plunge into, or simply exhibit in unblinking imagery, the action or argument.

In "Marrakech," he presents a series of sketches that segue into an inquiry into the depersonalizing that underlies imperialism and expresses both its absurdity and instability. Here's how the first sketch opens:

As the corpse went past the flies left the restaurant table in a cloud and rushed after it, but they came back a few minutes later.[5]

The flies are everywhere. They follow the burial procession because the "corpses here are never put into coffins." The burial grounds are a "huge waste of hummocky earth" without headstones so that "after a month or two no one can even be certain where his own relatives are buried."[6] This introductory sketch then announces its theme.

When you walk through a town like this—two hundred thousand inhabitants, of whom at least twenty thousand own literally nothing except the rags they stand up in—when you see how the people live, and still more how easily they die, it is always difficult to believe that you are walking among human beings. All colonial empires are in reality founded upon that fact.[7]

Here's how he opens "Shooting an Elephant."

In Moulmein, in Lower Burma, I was hated by large numbers of people—the only time in my life that I have been important enough for this to happen to me.[8]

He was "sub-divisional police officer of the town, and in an aimless, petty kind of way anti-European feeling was very bitter." The dynamics of that relationship are the subject of the essay. "All I knew was that I was stuck between my hatred of the empire I served and my rage against the evil spirited little beasts who tried to make my job impossible." The piece pivots around an event in which, he, the nominal authority, is chivvied by the yellow faces into needlessly shooting an elephant "solely to avoid looking a fool." Such is the preposterous foundation of imperial rule.[9]

A grimmer example comes from "A Hanging," which opens by moving from the general place (Burma) and mood ("sickly light") to the specifics of a jail for condemned men.

It was in Burma, a sodden morning of the rains. A sickly light, like yellow tinfoil, was slanting over the high walls into the jail yard. We were waiting outside the condemned cells, a row of sheds fronted with double bars, like small animal cages. Each cell measured about ten feet by ten and was quite bare within except for a plank bed and a pot of drinking water. In some of them brown silent men were squatting at the inner bars, with their blankets draped round them. These were the condemned men, due to be hanged within the next week or two.[10]

What follows are further specifics—the graphic, painful details of a particular man and how he is hanged, and because he did not go willingly there were complications (requiring warders to pull his legs while he dangled from the rope). The effect is to show the debasement that imperialism imposes not only on the ruled but on the rulers. The critique of colonialism is not based on first principles of political philosophy but on what actually must happen to enforce British presence on a people that don't want it. It's a commentary disguised as a story. The opening moves us into the setting of what follows. It needs no further gloss.

John McPhee, *Oranges*

The custom of drinking orange juice with breakfast is not very widespread, taking the world as a whole, and it is thought by many peoples to be a distinctly American habit. But many Danes drink it regularly with breakfast, and so do Hondurans, Filipinos, Jamaicans, and the wealthier citizens of Trinidad and Tobago. The day is started with orange juice in the Colombian Andes, and, to some extent, in Kuwait. Bolivians don't touch it at breakfast time, but they drink it steadily for the rest of the day. The "play lunch," or morning tea, that Australian children carry with them to school is usually an orange, peeled spirally halfway down, with the peel replaced around the fruit. The child unwinds the peel and holds the orange as if it were an ice-cream cone. People in Nepal almost never peel oranges, preferring to eat them in cut quarters, the way American athletes do. The sour oranges of Afghanistan customarily appear as seasoning agents on Afghan dinner tables. Squeezed over Afghan food, they cut the grease. The Shamouti Orange, of Israel, is seedless and sweet, has a thick skin, and grows in Hadera, Gaza, Tiberias, Jericho, the Jordan Valley, and Jaffa; it is exported from Jaffa, and for that reason is known universally beyond Israel as the Jaffa Orange. The Jaffa Orange is the variety that British people consider superior to all others, possibly because Richard the Lionhearted spent the winter of 1191–92 in the citrus groves of Jaffa. Citrus trees are spread across the North African coast from Alexandria to Tangier, the city whose name was given to tangerines. Oranges tend to become less tart the closer they are grown to the equator, and in Brazil there is one kind of orange that has virtually no acid in it at all. In the principal towns of Trinidad and Tobago, oranges are sold on street corners. The vender cuts them in half and sprinkles salt on them. In Jamaica, people halve oranges, get down on their hands and knees, clean floors with one half in each hand. Jamaican mechanics use oranges to clear away grease and oil. The blood orange of Spain, its flesh streaked with red, is prized throughout Europe. Blood oranges grow well in Florida, but they frighten American women. Spain has about thirty-five million orange trees, grows six billion oranges a year, and exports more oranges than any other country, including the United States. In the Campania region of Italy, land is scarce; on a typical small patch, set on a steep slope, orange trees are interspersed with olive and walnut trees, and grapes are trained to cover trellises overhead, and as many as five different vegetables are grown on the ground below. The over-all effect is that a greengrocer's shop is springing out of the hillside. Italy produces more than four billion oranges a year, but most of its citrus industry is scattered in gardens of one or two acres. A Frenchman sits at the dinner table, and, as the finishing flourish of the meal, slowly and gently disrobes an orange. In France, peeling the fruit is not yet considered an inconvenience. French preferences run to the blood oranges and the Thomson Navels of Spain, and to the thick-skinned, bland *Maltaises*, which the French import not from Malta but from Tunisia. France itself only grows about four hundred thousand oranges each year, almost wholly in the Department of the *Alpes Maritimes*. Sometimes, Europeans eat oranges with knives and forks. On occasion, they serve a dessert orange that has previously been peeled with such extraordinary care that strips of the peel arc outward like the petals of a flower from the separated and reassembled segments in the center. The Swiss sometimes serve oranges under a smothering of sugar and whipped cream; on a hot day in a Swiss garden, orange juice with ice is a luxurious drink. Norwegian children like to remove the top of an orange, make a little hole, push a lump of sugar into it, and then suck out the juice. English children make orange-peel teeth and wedge them over their gums on Halloween. Irish children take oranges to the movies, where they eat them while they watch the show, tossing peels at each other and at the people on the screen. In Reykjavik, Iceland, in green houses that are heated by volcanic springs, orange trees yearly bear fruit. In the New York Botanical Garden, six mature orange trees are growing in the soil of the Bronx. Their trunks are six inches in diameter, and they bear well every year. The oranges are for viewing and are not supposed to be picked. When people walk past them, however, they sometimes find them irresistible.[11]

It's the kind of paragraph that could give elementary-school English teachers fits. One fact tumbles into another like scree down a mountainside. There is no apparent topic sentence. Reading is like strolling past a cabinet of curiosities that lacks an obvious principle of organization. Yet the peeling back and serving up of facts, like that of preparing oranges, has its appeal. Whether bewildered or gasping to know how to connect all the tidbits, you keep reading. Instead of progressing from one topic to another, like a train of waves washing ashore, the endless roster becomes a rip tide that washes over and carries the reader.

What grabs is the unexpected organization. What holds attention is the flow of unexpected facts and the matter-of-fact telling of them, mostly free of connecting prose clutter, which suggests that the author does have a vision, if not a topic sentence, and the reader can trust him to reveal all at the end. Clearly, there is more to the orange than something to drink at breakfast. The long paragraph with its literary montage in place of normal transitions works like a movie trailer to tempt the reader to want more.

John McPhee, *Rising from the Plains*

This is about high-country geology and a Rocky Mountain regional geologist. I raise that semaphore here at the start so no one will feel misled by an opening passage in which a slim young woman who is not in any sense a geologist steps down from a train in Rawlins, Wyoming, in order to go north by stagecoach into country that was still very much the Old West. She arrived in the autumn of 1905, when she was twenty-three. Her hair was so blond it looked white. In Massachusetts, a few months before, she had graduated from Wellesley College and had been awarded a Phi Beta Kappa key, which now hung from a chain around her neck. Her field was classical studies. In addition to her skills in Latin and Greek, she could handle a horse expertly, but never had she made a journey into a region so remote as the one that lay before her.

Meanwhile, Rawlins surprised her: Rawlins, where shootings had once been so frequent that there seemed to be—as citizens put it—"a man for breakfast every morning"; Rawlins, half way across a state that was spending per annum far more to kill wolves and coyotes than to support its nineteen-year-old university. She had expected a "backward" town, a "frontier" town, a street full of badmen like Big Nose George, the road agent, the plunderer of stagecoaches, who signed his hidden-treasure maps "B. N. George." Instead, this October evening, she was met at the station by a lackey with a handcart, who wheeled her luggage to the Ferris Hotel. A bellboy took over, his chest a constellation of buttons. The place was three stories high, and cozy with steam heat. The lights were electric. There were lace curtains. What does it matter, she reflected, if the pitchers lack spouts?[12]

The opening creates interest not only by breaking the usual rhythms and expectations but by McPhee's announcing at the onset that he is deliberately doing so. This is a book about Rocky Mountain geology for which geologist David Love will serve as McPhee's guide. The

Wellesley graduate in the opening is Love's mother. The unfolding story is full of unexpected events, some seemingly overturned, not unlike the great Overthrust Belt that unconventionally rammed older strata atop younger and bewildered a generation of naturalists. The task of the regional geologist is to unravel that narrative snarl from rock outcrops and roadcuts. John McPhee does not recapitulate so much as re-create the saga of that decipherment as bits of history, often chronically scrambled, present themselves.

The text opens with a classic Old West theme: the coming of civilization to the wild. That the woman is unnamed adds to the generic quality of the formula. But the West she finds is different from what she expected, and so it will be with the history that follows. What, from a craft perspective, invests this particular introduction with interest is the fact that McPhee tells us the opening anecdote is in effect a piece of misdirection. That confession allows him to have his story and its Old West ambience and then segue into his profile of David Love.

V. S. Pritchett, "The Despot": A Book Review of a Biography of Tolstoy

The life of Tolstoy is a novel that might have been written by Aksakov in its beginning, by Gogol in the middle and by Dostoevsky in the years following the conversion. He is not so much a man as a collection of double-men, each driven by enormous energy and, instinctively, to extremes. A difficulty for the biographer is that while we grin at the sardonic comedy of Tolstoy's contradictions and are stunned by his blind egotism, we are also likely to be infected by his exaltation: how is this exclamatory life to be brought to earth and to be distributed into its hours and days? And besides this there is the crucial Russian difficulty which the Russian novel revels in and which mystifies ourselves: there seems to be no such person as a Russian alone. Each one appears in a crowd of relations and friends, an extravagantly miscellaneous and declaiming tribal court. At Yasnaya Polyana the house was like an inn or caravanserai. There is no question of avoiding Tolstoy as a case or a collection of arguments. And the final affront to biography is the fact that Tolstoy exhaustively presented his life nakedly in his works.[13]

This a lot to pack into one paragraph: it is not so much a hook as a string of hooks; if a reader passes one baited hook, there is quickly another. It almost recapitulates its subject, beginning as one kind of statement and cascading into a crowd of others. Clearly, the right audience is critical for such a passage to carry a theme. It coaxes through an appeal to intellectual curiosity. It speaks to readers already versed in classic literature, particularly Russian. If the reader doesn't understand the references, the piece will be gibberish. For those who pick up the allusions, the rapid pace and multiple references hold interest. Leo Tolstoy is a cameo of Russia.

This cascade may be the element of craft that holds the greatest interest. If Pritchett had used one reference, or devoted one sentence to each in turn, along with a complementary sentence to elaborate and explain its meaning, the paragraph would drag. Instead, while teetering on confusion, it rumbles along, carried by an infectious exaltation for the subject. This may also be a case where clarity must yield to meaning. A writer, editor, or reader for whom directness and simplicity are the supreme virtues would recoil from such a rush. But a knowledgeable reader, or one eager to learn, might well be caught up in this intellectual stream of consciousness and want to continue to have the pieces parsed separately.

V. S. Pritchett, "The Performing Lynx": Review of Saki, *The Unbearable Bassington*

"I'm living so far beyond my income," says one of the characters in Saki's *The Unbearable Bassington*, "that we may almost be said to be living apart." That is a pointer to Saki's case: it is the fate of wits to live beyond the means of their feeling. They live by dislocation and extravagance. They talk and tire in the hard light of brilliance and are left frightened and alone among the empty wine-glasses and tumbled napkins of the wrecked dinner-table. Saki was more than a wit. There was silence in him as well. In that silence one sees a freak of the traveling show of story-tellers, perhaps a gifted performing animal, and it is wild. God knows what terrors and cajoleries have gone on behind the scenes to produce this gifted lynx so contemptuously consenting to be half-human. But one sees the hankering after one last ferocious act in the cause of a nature abused. The peculiar character called Keriway who crops up unexplained in the middle of the Bassington novel tells the story of a "tame, crippled crane." "It was lame," Keriway says, "that is why it was tame."

What lamed and what tamed Saki?[14]

Another seemingly crowded paragraph. By normal standards it should have two, maybe three topic sentences, but the variety is what gives the passage its motivating energy, as the biographical tensions animated Saki. In Pritchett's Tolstoy profile, Tolstoy stands for and takes on the vastness and confusion of Russia. In his Saki sketch, Saki is a means to characterize a class of people who lack a particular place to roost, who must live by their wits. After this provocative sketch, Pritchett poses his theme, and most readers will want to read on to learn how Saki was lamed and tamed. The appeal is not to an audience already versed in a general literature but to one curious to know about this freak-show oddity of a writer.

"The *Economist* Takes Sir Wilfred Thesiger to Lunch: 'The Last Explorer's Last Journey'"

The second thing you notice about Sir Wilfred Thesiger is the shoes—vast, lumpy things like gnarled tree roots, glowing with years of loving care and ox-blood polish. "I can't remember how old they are," he growls. Cobbler-made by Lobb's of St James's Street, London, of course. If you have walked the Danikil in Ethiopia, crossed the Empty Quarter of Arabia on foot, wandered around Sudan, climbed the Hindu Kush, trekked in northern Kenya and fought with the SAS in the Western Desert, shoes are important.

But the first thing that strikes you about Thesiger (somehow Sir Wilfred sounds too feeble) are the eyes; granite grey, tiny and set a mile deep each side of a broken, hawk's beak nose. It is a great face—people stop in the street and stare at the tall stooping but powerfully built figure. He does not smile much. But the eyes sparkle with fun when he orders "that sweet, brown, fizzy drink they like in Kenya." Coca-Cola? "Yes that stuff." Can there be a greater symbol of everything Thesiger has fought against for all of his 87 years than Coca-Cola? "I suppose so. I don't care. I rather like it."[15]

The inverted sequencing—the second following the first—does two things. It creates suspense, and because it focuses on shoes it allows the writer to introduce the basic travels that define Thesiger's career without interrupting the flow of what will follow. The choice of the two "things" is not arbitrary: they are both telling details that reveal story and character. Ending with a bottle of Coke helps sharpen the depiction of Thesiger as a man of a previous era. That he—Thesiger—chooses it anyway speaks to his sense of himself and willingness to act as he chooses however outsiders might regard it.

What saves the opening from the status of a literary stunt is that fact that everything that follows in the profile flows from these two brief paragraphs. It isn't simply that the surprising introduction gets the reader's attention. It uses that attention to nail down the critical character of Sir Wilfred.

Opening as Informing Image

Wilfred Thesiger, *Arabian Sands*

So now let Sir Wilfred try his hand at some of the informing experiences that made him.

A cloud gathers, the rain falls, men live; the cloud disperses without rain, and men and animals die. In the deserts of southern Arabia there is no rhythm of the seasons, no rise and fall of sap, but empty wastes where only the changing temperature marks the passage of the year. It is a bitter, desiccated land which knows nothing of gentleness or ease. Yet men have lived there since earliest times. Passing generations have left fire-blackened stones at camping sites, a few faint tracks polished on the gravel plains. Elsewhere the winds wipe out their footprints. Men live there because it is the world into which they were born; the life they lead is the life their forefathers led before them; they accept hardships and privations; they know no other way. Lawrence wrote in *Seven Pillars of Wisdom*, "Bedouin ways were hard, even for those brought up in them and for strangers terrible: a death in life." No man can live this life and emerge unchanged. He will carry, however faint, the imprint of the desert, the brand which marks the nomad; and he will have within him the yearning to return, weak or insistent according to his nature. For this cruel land can cast a spell which no temperate clime can match.[16]

The opening sentence, as unblinking as the desert sun, is a perfect entree to the theme that follows. The Empty Quarter is a world without the usual order of temperate climates (which characterize much of Europe), and over which there is no human control, so it seems fitting that the passage lacks the usual rhythms of argument or thesis, and hinges on a paradox, that in this intrinsically inimical land people live and that such lives matter even to those who only pass through the great emptiness.

A stark land, a stoic life, a monosyllabic prose. The brevity and singularity of the interpretive vision, like the sudden dawn of the desert, illuminates and startles and draws us on. If *Oranges* animates readers by its overflowing details, *Arabian Sands* inspires them with its brevity and prose polished as though by wind-blown sand.

Opening as Set Piece

Barbara Tuchman, *The Guns of August* (1962)

A master of the grand narrative, Barbara Tuchman found in the early omens and opening events of the Great War a subject to match her style. The inaugural chapter to *The Guns of August* could stand as an exemplary text for openings, settings, and just plain classy narrative. "The Funeral" portrays a lush spectacle, which segues into a deep suspicion: the two act like scissors to cut the past and set the stage for the future.

So gorgeous was the spectacle on the May morning of 1910 when nine kings rode in the funeral of Edward VII of England that the crowd, waiting in hushed and black-clad awe, could not keep back gasps of admiration. In scarlet and blue and green and purple, three by three the sovereigns rode through the palace gates, with plumed helmets, gold braid, crimson sashes, and jeweled orders flashing in the sun. After them came five heirs apparent, forty more imperial or royal highnesses, seven queens—four dowager and three regnant—and a scattering of special ambassadors from uncrowned countries. Together they represented seventy nations in the greatest assemblage of royalty and rank ever gathered in one place and, of its kind, the last. The muffled tongue of Big Ben tolled nine by the clock as the cortege left the palace, but on history's clock it was sunset, and the sun of the old world was setting in a dying blaze of splendor never to be seen again.

In the center of the front row rode the new king, George V, flanked on his left by the Duke of Connaught, the late king's only surviving brother, and on his right by a personage to whom, acknowledged *The Times*, "belongs the first place among all the foreign mourners," who "even when relations are most strained has never lost his popularity amongst us"—William II, the German Emperor. Mounted on a gray horse, wearing the scarlet uniform of a British Field Marshal, carrying the baton of that rank, the Kaiser had composed his features behind the famous upturned mustache in an expression "grave even to severity." Of the several emotions churning his susceptible breast, some hints exist in his letters. "I am proud to call this place my home and to be a member of this royal family," he wrote home after spending the night in Windsor Castle in the former apartments of his mother. Sentiment and nostalgia induced by these melancholy occasions with his English relatives jostled with pride in his supremacy among the assembled potentates and with a fierce relish in the disappearance of his uncle from the European scene. He had come to bury Edward his bane; Edward the arch plotter, as William conceived it, of Germany's encirclement; Edward his mother's brother whom he could neither bully nor impress, whose fat figure cast a shadow between Germany and the sun. "He is Satan. You cannot imagine what a Satan he is!"[17]

Part of the effect lies in the basic design: the pageant and the panorama are old devices for surveying a historical scene. Here is the proverbial pride before the fall. In this case the parade has the added value of personalizing larger processes, which literally pass in review. The temperaments of the protagonists match that of the times. But the other part is the quiet authority of a voice that does not need to hyperventilate its rhetoric.

There is nothing flashy about the prose. It moves with the stately pace of the funeral itself. What elevates the text are the buried contrasts of opulence and death; the sibling-like rivalry between England's and Germany's leaders; the parallelisms with which William II imagines Edward VII; and the bitter quote that concludes the portrait. Let William II make the startling declarations. The job of the author is to select the right quotes and insert them into the right place.

The book concludes, after the trauma of the Great War, with Emile Verhaeren, who dedicates a poem to "the man I used to be." The world that passed in review in 1910 is no longer recognizable to those who look over the wreckage left at the war's end.

Opening as Thesis

Isaiah Berlin, "Does Political Theory Still Exist?," "The Pursuit of the Ideal," "The Concept of Scientific History," *The Proper Study of Mankind*

Surprise openings work because they lie outside the norm. But if everyone works against the grain, the punch of the prose itself must replace surprise as a means of engaging attention. Like people who choose not to vaccinate but rely for their immunity on the fact that the rest of the community does, so writers who shun the usual formulas depend on those who hold to them.

There is no reason, however, that stock openings must be boring or clunky. Like any writing they can be done well or poorly. The directly posed thesis can be riveting, however plainly stated, if the topic is powerful and its presentation engaging. A master essayist like Isaiah Berlin shows how to do it.

Here he opens with the informing question and lays out the terms of inquiry.

Is there still such a subject as political theory? This query, put with suspicious frequency in English-speaking countries, questions the very credentials of the subject: it suggests that political philosophy, whatever it may have been in the past, is today dead or dying. The principal symptom which seems to support this belief is that no commanding work of political philosophy has appeared in the twentieth century. By a commanding work in the field of general ideas I mean at the very least one that has in a large area converted paradoxes into platitudes or vice versa. This seems to me no more (but also no less) than an adequate criterion of the characteristic in question.[18]

What follows is an extended argument, rigorously but accessibly written. Here he opens by identifying two phenomena and tracing out their curious bond and consequences.

There are, in my view, two factors that, above all others, have shaped human history in the twentieth century. One is the development of the natural sciences and technology, certainly the greatest success story of our time—to this, great and mounting attention has been paid from all quarters. The other, without doubt, consists in the great ideological storms that have altered the lives of virtually all mankind: the Russian Revolution and its aftermath—totalitarian tyrannies of both right and left and the explosions of nationalism, racism, and, in places, religious bigotry which, interestingly enough, not one among the most perceptive social thinkers of the nineteenth century had ever predicted.[19]

Not a grabber for readers habituated to *People* magazine, but for an audience of peers, intellectuals all, there is little need for preambles and windy perorations. Such readers will continue because they find the topic compelling or because they just want to hear Berlin reason through it.

In this final example, Berlin eases his query into "the concept of scientific history" with a touch of personification (but then his theme is about history as individuals).

History, according to Aristotle, is an account of what individual human beings have done and suffered. In a still wider sense, history is what historians do. Is history then a natural science, as, let us say, physics or biology or psychology are sciences? And if not, should it seek to be one? And if it fails to be one, what prevents it? Is this due to human error or impotence, or to the nature of the subject, or does the very problem rest on a confusion between the concept of history and that of natural science? These have been questions that have occupied the minds of both philosophers and philosophically minded historians at least since the beginning of the nineteenth century, when men became self-conscious about the purpose and logic of their intellectual activities. But two centuries before that Descartes had already denied to history any claim to be a serious study. Those who accepted the validity of the Cartesian criterion of what constitutes rational method could (and did) ask how they could find the clear and simple elements of which historical judgments were composed, and into which they could be analysed: where were the definitions, the logical transformation rules, the rules of inference, the rigorously deduced conclusions? While the accumulation of this confused amalgam of memories and travelers' tales, fables and chroniclers' stories, moral reflections and gossip might be a harmless pastime, it was beneath the dignity of serious men seeking what alone is worth seeking—the discovery of the truth in accordance with principles and rules which alone guarantee scientific validity.[20]

Contemporary editors would probably break that passage into three paragraphs, and only a specialized journal would publish it, but that does not mean it is badly written or unworthy of emulation. What it does, it does brilliantly. Literary nonfiction doesn't mean simply rhetorical flourishes and human-interest drama: it means matching the style of expression with what is being expressed. Berlin's essay is an argument—an assay, in its original meaning—to be tested by evidence, logic, and persuasive prose. The literary question here is how well he matches subject and style. Here an august theme gets an august text.

Opening as Narrative Prologue

Simon Schama, *Citizens*

Simon Schama's *Citizens* is an unapologetically old-school grand narrative of the French Revolution, and "both the form of its telling and its chosen subject matter represent a deliberate turning away from analytical history towards Events and Persons, both long forbidden, or dismissed as mere froth on the great waves of history. It is a narrative not by default but by choice. . . ." The narrative form requires that the opening be not merely enticing but organically linked to the ending. What is announced must be answered.[21]

In this case the style of the opening prologue is a cameo of the text overall: it comes with its own internal beginning, middle, and end. It starts with the story of a plaster elephant intended by Napoleon to represent "the superiority of imperial conquest over chaotic insurrection." As the elephant ("a sorry spectacle") is moved, redefined, and remade or left to rot, it comes to stand for the changing memories of the Revolution. An unexpected symbol, it moves the wondering reader through the subsequent revolutions of interpretation, leading to *Citizens*. The rest of the prologue pivots on the contrast of two figures from the era who both return in 1830 for a commemoration of sorts. Gilbert de Lafayette stands for the idealism and aspirations of the revolutionary generation. Maurice de Talleyrand represents the practical survivor, moving from the ancien régime to the new order of capitalism without misstep. Yet together, "in their own persons, Lafayette and Talleyrand embodied the split personality of the French Revolution." The world was the product of their irreconcilable interests. "The fiction of the Revolution was to imagine that each might be served without damaging the other and its history amounts to the realization of that impossibility."[22]

Schama then argues against reflexive irony, which in the case of the Revolution, and as the Revolution did with its founders, turns on itself. The ironist Talleyrand seduced Mme Delacroix, who gave birth to Eugene Delacroix, whose painting, *Liberty Leading the People*, came to epitomize the remembered Revolution. Thus the "greatest Romantic of the new age [was] sired by the most formidable skeptic of the old." What renders irony inadequate is that the contrasting visions were in fact not separate but joined in an "imperfect union."[23]

So, too, the organizing principle of the text is not a thesis but a theme made flesh by its representation in people and related through their stories. The prologue thus introduces not only Schama's themes but also the style of his presentation, which is a thick description that explains less through logical argument than by a kind of literary envelopment. The coup de grace comes with the epilogue, in which the various topics and characters introduced in the prologue find closure.

2

Resetting the Scene

In which we explore ways in which a text becomes a context through placing events, buildings, people, and ideas into a setting.

C ontext matters. In fact, context and contingency are what historical understanding brings to a subject: they help make stories into narratives. It's possible to just state those conditions. ("Three factors contributed to the events that followed. The first. . . .") But it is also possible to show them. It might take the form of a building or landscape that expresses the intentions and circumstances of its creator. Or a social group that fashions and sustains the values of a protagonist. Or the geographic or political setting that channels action or deflects behavior the way a massive star can capture a comet.

In brief, not all settings are dumb or interchangeable, a common stage that can be furnished for particular human actions of the current script. Some help write the script. Some become part of a supporting cast. Some so claim the center that they organize the action and inform its interpretation. It is possible to describe such settings in the drab language of factors and contributing causes and to relegate settings to the wallpaper of history. It's also possible, as the examples below demonstrate, to let settings join in the action. They may not be characters, but they can, in a literary function, act as characters in the text, demanding the same attention to telling details and selective portraiture and thickening a reader's appreciation. Ambience matters.

Instead of background data—setting the stage for action—a well-crafted scene can move along with the action. It can be a symbol, an informing principle, a presence that directs behavior. It can add meaning, not just information. It can be as memorable as human actors and narrated events.

Built Landscape as Expression of Human Values

Henry Adams, *Mont Saint Michel and Chartres*

Not much question here what grips Henry Adams's imagination: art as an expression of an age, Saint Michael the Archangel as a symbol of Norman energy, the church of Saint Michiel de la Mer del Peril as the expression of their fusion. The text opens with a declaration like a sudden visitation.

The Archangel loved heights. Standing on the summit of the tower that crowned his church, wings upspread, sword uplifted, the devil crawling beneath, and the cock, symbol of eternal vigilance, perched on his mailed foot, Saint Michael held a place of his own in heaven and on earth which seems, in the eleventh century, to leave hardly room for the Virgin of the Crypts at Chartres, still less for the Beau Christ of the thirteenth century at Amiens. The Archangel stands for Church and State, and both militant. He is the conqueror of Satan, the mightiest of all created spirits, the nearest to God. His place was where the danger was greatest; therefore you find him here. For the same he was, while the pagan danger lasted, the patron Saint of France. So the Normans, when they were converted to Christianity, put themselves under his powerful protection. So he stood for centuries on his Mount in Peril of the Sea, watching across the tremor of the immense ocean,—*immensi tremor oceani*,—as Louis XI, inspired for once to poetry, inscribed on the collar of the Order of Saint Michael which he created. So soldiers, nobles, and monarchs went on pilgrimage to his shrine. So the common people followed, and still follow, like ourselves.[1]

Such heights of significance and power deserve settings that embody those sentiments. The complex of buildings takes on the character of a statue, and can be analyzed as such.

The church stands high on the summit of this granite rock, and on its west front is the platform, to which the tourist ought first to climb. From the edge of this platform, the eye plunges down, two hundred and thirty-five feet, to the wide sands or the wider ocean, as the tides recede or advance, under an infinite sky, over a restless sea which even we tourists can understand and feel without books or guides; but when we turn from the western view, and look at the church door, thirty or forty yards from the parapet where we stand, one needs to be eight centuries old to know what this mass of encrusted architecture meant to its builders, and even then one must still learn to feel it. The man who wanders into the twelfth century is lost, unless he can grow prematurely young.[2]

In this inaugural image, everything points upward and to a society organized on principles similar to its theology.

Perched on the extreme point of this abrupt rock, the Church militant with its aspirant Archangel stands high above the world, and seems to threaten heaven itself. The idea is the stronger and more restless because the Church of Saint Michael is surrounded and protected by the world and the society over which it rises, as Duke William rested on his barons and their men. Neither the Saint nor the Duke was troubled by doubts about his mission. Church and State, Soul and Body, God and Man, are all one at Mont Saint Michel, and the business of all is to fight, each in his own way, or to stand guard for each other. Neither Church nor State is intellectual, or learned, or even strict in dogma. Here we do not feel the Trinity at all; the Virgin but little; Christ hardly more; we feel only the Archangel and the Unity of God. We have little logic here, and simple faith, but we have energy. We cannot do many things which are done in the center of civilization, at Byzantium, but we can fight, and we can build a church.[3]

But the design reflected the age of a Church Militant and, as the initial construction spread outward, it became increasingly unstable: aspiration alone could not hold it together; the Abbot Hildebert "asked too much of it." Times changed, the Crusades faltered, fashions faded, and later efforts to elaborate on that initial vision began to spall apart. One of the towers collapsed in 1300, along with crusading zeal. In 1618, seventy-five years after Copernicus published *De Revolutionibus*, which put another vision at the center, and sixty-nine years before Newton brought out the *Principia Mathematica*, the facade gave way. In 1776, at the start of the age of democratic revolutions, three of the seven spans of the nave were "pulled down." So human history is recorded in its buildings as well as its annals.[4]

Later contrasts with Chartres, inspired (as Adams sees it) by a Church Triumphant, and so sited in a plain and outfitted with features like a great roseate more befitting another time whose great enthusiasms filled the vessel of the Virgin. Still later in a famous essay Adams contrasts the power of the Virgin, as expressed in Chartres, with the power of the Corliss engine, the artifact of an age of coal and steam. Ideas can assume, under human hands, a material expression beyond words, and that later words reflect upon.

Place Affecting Human Character

Wallace Stegner, *Mormon Country*

Because he analyzes things made by people, Adams operates within the realm of art criticism, or at least of artifact criticism. One can disagree with his interpretations—there is no autonomous standard for judging art, after all—and one can like (or dislike) his prose, but the idea of using the built landscape as a proxy for cultural beliefs and values is an accepted one. The relation between natural settings is trickier, both in its intellectual premise and its translation into words.

Here Wallace Stegner distills what he regards as the essence of the Great Basin. The sketch belongs with a suite that defines the limits of what he terms "Mormon Country."

Three or four little puddles, an interminable string of crazy, warped, arid mountains with broad valleys swung between them; a few water-holes, a few springs, a few oasis towns and a few dry towns dependent for water on barrels and horsepower; a few little valleys where irrigation is possible and where the alfalfa looks incredibly green as you break down out of the pass; a desert more vegetationless, more indubitably hot and dry, and more terrible than any desert in North America except possibly Death Valley; an uncounted wealth of minerals—gold, silver, lead, zinc, copper, mercury, antimony—that about sums up the Great Basin. Its rivers run nowhere but into the ground; its lakes are probably salty or brackish; its rainfall is negligible and its scenery depressing to all but the few who have lived in it long enough to acquire a new set of values about scenery. Its snake population is large and its human population small. Its climate shows extremes of temperature that would tire out anything but a very strong thermometer. It is a dead land, though a very rich one. Even the Mormons could do little with it. They settled its few watered valleys and let the rest of it alone. The Gentiles swarmed into its mining camps and when the leads petered out they swarmed out again. Even in terms of towns, the dead in the Great Basin outnumber its living.[5]

The telling details come first, capped by the organizing theme ("that about sums up the Great Basin"). A series of parallel sentences then elaborate on those features which make the landscape formidable to humans. Then comes an explicit evaluation for what these conditions meant to the two kinds of Americans, Mormons and Gentiles, who moved into the area, not in abstract terms but as measured by how they responded. The Mormons stayed, a little. The Gentiles left. A final characterization of the Great Basin takes the form not of theses or counterarguments or general principles of historical geography but of a concrete image. The dead outnumber the living.

This is a character profile of a place. Probably its concluding statement could be considered a testable hypothesis, but to what end? Stegner's portrait leaves the reader with a vivid image of the western borders to a pattern of settlement, which is to say, of a culture and its way of life. Like a character introduced in a big narrative, the sketch stays with the reader, who can conjure it up whenever "Great Basin" reappears later in the text.

Setting as Index of Historical Developments

Harold Lamb, *Hannibal: One Man Against Rome*

Stegner's depiction of the Great Basin pits the character of a place against the character of a people. In his biography of Hannibal, Harold Lamb uses a simple account of geography to explicate the motives and maneuverings of two emerging empires. No rhetorical flights here, just the basic facts of the Mediterranean clearly laid out in declarative sentences in what Lamb calls "the testimony of the Sea." The chronicle pauses, while the sea speaks. The regional geography organizes what otherwise tends to be a confusing, even cross-purposed welter of events. Lamb might have inserted himself at his point, laying out his arguments in the persona of omniscient historian, but by refracting his views through a map he gives his observations a visual, concrete image. The geography does not so much determine the cause of events as pare them into more understandable statements. Lamb's task is to parse it in ways that allow for clarity without oversimplification.

The waters of the Middle Sea itself might have told the true cause of what began in the year 219. For this was the climax of the struggle of 120 years for mastery of those waters by two avid and pitiless human powers.

An invisible line, of course, had always divided the south of the Middle Sea from the north. It divided the continental mass of Africa from Europe, the Libyan-Semitic-Egyptian inhabitants from the Aryan invaders who swept over the Greek peninsula and the lovely island of Crete. Phoenicians of the south had joined with Persians of the east against the Dorian Greeks. There was still little in common between the dwellers on the southern coast and those on the northern. Eratosthenes (as geographer) had just drawn his main axis of the Mediterranean, through the Strait of Gibraltar and Sicily above the island of Rhodes. The coasts themselves were entirely different. In the north miniature seas lay between peninsulas; great rivers drained the hinterland; sheltered bays invited ships, while island chains led toward distant shores. On the south the forbidding African coast stretched interminably, with almost no harbors and with the outlet of only one great river, the Nile....

The Middle Sea had one junction point where the divided coasts all but touched, where the long peninsula of Italy extended across the narrow Strait of Messina to Sicily, the western tip of which lay less than 125 miles from Carthage. This land barrier in turn separated the large eastern half of the Mediterranean from the western half....

The two halves fought for supremacy. The Carthaginians seized "mastery of the western Mediterranean." Yet "the cultured eastern Mediterranean had growing need of the raw materials of the barbaric west," and "after the turn of the third century, the attempt of Pyrrhus, soldier-king of Epirus, to carve out an empire through southern Italy and Sicily—the prosperous Magna Graecia—was a consequence of economic need." It was also prompted by "the first appearance of Roman ships off the free city of Tarentum." So the third and final party, Rome, enters the contest. "When the brilliant Pyrrhus was at last defeated by Roman legions (275) and left the shores of Italy, legend makes him say: 'What a fine battlefield

I am leaving to the Romans and Carthaginians.' Probably he never said it, but it turned out to be true."[6]

This is far from riveting prose, but it is remarkably clear, and completely readable, and the point of interest—for us—is the authorial strategy of stepping back from the text and finding a usable way to untangle a complex narrative. In this case, Lamb appeals to regional geography, as in another setting an author might assume to speak through the pose of an omniscient commentator, or refract those views by turning to another historian for quotes, or to a participant or a chronicler from the time. In fact, Lamb does just this with the concluding observation from Pyrrhus. And in what may be the most innovative bit of craft in the entire passage, he finds a way to cope with a potentially troubled quote without straying outside the lines of nonfiction.

G. V. Trevelyan, *A Shortened History of England*

Another simple example: here G. V. Trevelyan refers to the history of maps to illustrate the history of England:

> The history of civilized man in our country is very old; it begins long before the reign of Alfred. But the history of Britain as a leader in the world's affairs is of much shorter date; it begins with the reign of Elizabeth. The reason can be read upon the map. Map-makers, whether in ancient Alexandria or in medieval monasteries, placed our island on the north-west edge of all things. But, after the discovery of America and the ocean routes to Africa and the East, Britain lay in the centre of the new maritime movement. This change in her geographic outlook was employed to good purpose by her inhabitants, who in the era of the Stuarts made her the chief seat of the new trans-oceanic commerce and of the finance and industry that sustained it....
>
> Britain has always owed her fortunes to the sea, and to the havens and rivers that from the earliest times opened her inland regions to what the sea might bring....[7]

Again, the map makes visual the author's thesis. Beyond that, classic parallelism and a change in tempo (in the form of sentence length: "The reason can be read upon a map") make for a sharp, memorable argument.

Geography Channeling History

David Crowley, *City of Fortune*

Now for a closer look at one of the seas that collectively compose the Mediterranean, in this case its informing significance for Venice:

> The Adriatic Sea is the liquid reflection of Italy, a tapering channel some 480 miles long and 100 wide, pinched tighter at its southern point where it flows into the Ionian past the island of Corfu. At its most northern point, in the enormous curved bay called the Gulf of Venice, the water is a curious blue-green. Here the river Po churns out tons of alluvial material from the distant Alps, which settle to form haunting stretches of lagoon and marsh. So great is the volume of these glacial deposits that the Po Delta is advancing fifteen feet a year and the ancient port of Adria, after which the sea is named, now lies fourteen miles inland.

The silting delta introduces geology, and Crowley expands that geology to explain geographic differences between the eastern and western Adriatic.

> Geology has made the Adriatic's two coasts quite distinct. The western, Italian shore is a curved, low-lying beach, which provides poor harbors but ideal landing spots for would-be invaders. Sail due east and your vessel will snub against limestone. The shores of Dalmatia and Albania are a four-hundred-mile stretch as the crow flies, but so deeply crenellated with sheltering covers, indents, offshore islands, reefs, and shoals that they comprise two thousand miles of intricate coast. Here are the sea's natural anchorages, which may shelter a whole fleet or conceal an ambush. Behind these features, sometimes stepped back by coastal

plain, sometimes hard down on the sea, stand the abrupt white lime-stone mountains that barricade the sea from the upland Balkans. The Adriatic is the frontier between two worlds.

Now Crowley moves from raw geology to what that geology means for history, all made vivid by the use of details of places and goods moved between them.

For thousands of years—from the early Bronze Age until well after the Portuguese rounded Africa—this fault line was a marine highway linking central Europe with the eastern Mediterranean, and a portal for world trade. Ships passed up and down the sheltering Dalmatian shore with the goods of Arabia, Germany, Italy, the Black Sea, India, and the farthest East. Over the centuries they carried Baltic amber to the burial chamber of Tutankhamen; blue faience beads from Mycenae to Stonehenge; Cornish tin to the smelters of the Levant; the spices of Malacca to the courts of France; Cotswold wool to the merchants of Cairo. Timber, slaves, cotton, copper, weapons, seeds, stories, inventions, and ideas sailed up and down these coasts. "It is astonishing," wrote a thirteenth-century Arab traveler about the cities of the Rhine, "that although this place is in the Far West, there are spices there which are to be found only in the Far East—pepper, ginger, clovers, spikenard, costus, and galanga, all in enormous quantities." They came up the Adriatic. This was the point where hundreds of arterial routes converged. From Britain and the North Sea, down the river Rhine, along beaten tracks through the Teutonic forests, across Alpine passes, mule trains threaded their way to the top of the gulf, where the merchandices of the East also landed. Here goods were transshipped and ports flourished; first Greek Adria, then Roman Aquileia, and finally Venice. In the Adriatic, site is everything: Adria silted up; Aquileia, on the coastal plain, was flattened by Attila the Hun in 452; Venice prospered in the aftermath because it was unreachable. Its smattering of low-lying muddy islets set in a malarial lagoon was separated from the mainland by a few precious miles of shallow water. This unpromising place would become the entrepôt and interpreter of worlds; the Adriatic, its passport.[8]

"Site is everything"—there is the essence of the passage; and everything should go to demonstrate that fact. Probably it doesn't matter that the Gulf of Venice is "blue-green," or that the Po delta is advancing fifteen feet a year. Nor do the lists of trade goods need to be enumerated twice, once by the author and again, partially, by the unnamed Arab traveler. What matters is the positioning of the Adriatic Sea between Europe and Asia Minor; the distinct character of the two shorelines, Italy's and Dalmatia's; the pairing of Corfu and Venice, as entries and entrepôts, the hinged doors that control movement; and the lagoons that define and defend Venice. The Adriatic is both buffer and bottleneck. Venice's lagoons can shield the city; but the trade upon which its wealth and power rest must extend to Corfu, and beyond.

David Crowley's description of Venice's natural setting thus maps the contours of its story. The narrative tides of Venetian history will slosh back and forth within the Adriatic.

Social Settings

A setting needn't be only geographic. It can be political, establishing the context for some event; or intellectual, helping place some idea or innovation; or social, a profile of a group. If the writer begins a book or chapter with such passages, they may be considered openings as well as settings. They set up the analysis or narrative to follow.

Richard Hofstadter, *The American Political Tradition*

In his chapter on Theodore Roosevelt as a politician, Richard Hofstadter opens with a profile of a class of men, of which Roosevelt was one.

The coarse, materialistic civilization that emerged in the United States during the years after the Civil War produced among cultivated middle-class young men a generation of alienated and homeless intellectuals. Generally well-to-do, often of eminent family backgrounds, clubmen, gentlemen, writers, the first cluster of a native intellectual aristocracy to appear since the great days of Boston and Concord, the men of this class found themselves unable to participate with any heart in the greedy turmoil of business or to accept without protest boss-ridden politics. Money-making was sordid; politics was dirty; and the most sensitive among them made their careers in other ways. Those who were less interested in public affairs usually managed to fit themselves into the interstices of American existence. Some, like Henry James, escaped abroad or, like his brother William, immersed themselves in academic life. One, Oliver Wendell Holmes, Jr., found sanctuary on the Massachusetts bench and at length rose to the Supreme Court; another, Henry Adams, made a sort of career of bitter detachment. Some who were strong enough to overcome their distaste for business entered it without finding much personal fulfillment and left without regret. Charles Francis Adams, Jr., upon retiring from an unhappy career as a railroad executive, observed that among all the tycoons he had met, "not one ... would I care to meet again in this world or the next; nor is one associated in my mind with the idea of humor, thought, or refinement."[9]

Classic rhetorical techniques, ending with a striking quote—the passage might have been written by Francis Parkman. The prose is precise and lively. The same argument could have been written as a straight thesis and Roosevelt's social class stated as part of background biography. Instead, as with Stegner's sketch, the passage creates a contrast, one sharpened by examples.

It's an opening, but of a particular sort in that it does not simply grab attention but sets up a social context—a class of men—out of which Theodore Roosevelt will emerge. It strengthens Roosevelt's achievement by showing what he was not or chose not to become. Where his social peers mostly stood outside the rough sport of politics and business, he would enter the fray. In the words of later, famous essays, he would refuse to be a mere "cumberer upon the earth's surface" but would take up a life of "strenuous endeavor." He would be "the man in the arena."

Hofstadter's chapter ends with Roosevelt determined to join the Great War until felled by a coronary embolism: the contrast between him and the class sketched at the opening continues. In fact, the chapter could have ended many ways and retained its theme. Hofstadter chose the war because it segues nicely into his next profile, that of Woodrow Wilson. In good writing, nothing just happens.

Setting Up Irony

Martha A. Sandweiss, *Passing Strange: A Gilded Age Tale of Love and Deception Across the Color Line* (2009)

For the past century irony has been the default voice of literature. Irony is a fact of the world, but that it has become the final resting point for so much serious literature is a fact of historical moment. There are plenty of reasons to believe it is time to move on, and few reasons to believe such movement will happen any time soon.

In *Passing Strange* Martha Sandweiss establishes irony as an informing voice in the prologue. By following a census taker in 1900, she can both capture rich details and create an ambience, all while imagining a conversation, which further grounds the context in concrete images. The scene becomes more fully realized. The irony sharpens not from vaporous declarations but from the disparity of recorded census replies and the reality of the lived life.

"Edward V. Brown, the census taker, moved slowly down North Prince Street, knocking on each and every door in this Flushing neighborhood of Queens, New York. It was June 5, 1900, a mild and sunny day in the first spring of a new century." He tallies the data required "in his careful, neat hand." Then he

> knocked at the large and comfortable home at 48 North Prince Street. Two black servants lived here. Phoebe Martin was a thirty-three-year-old widow, and Clarine Eldridge, just fourteen, was scarcely older than the children she had been hired to watch. It was afternoon, and Grace, age nine; Ada, age eight; and Sidney, age six, were home from school, perhaps playing with their three-year-old brother, Wallace. Whoever answered the door probably invited the census taker into the parlor; nether the servants nor the children could have answered his long list of personal questions about the family. And so Edward Brown entered the home to talk to Ada Todd, the lady of the house. Her husband, James, was away, she said, so she would answer the census agent's long list of questions herself.
>
> Brown hardly needed to ask her race. He wrote "black" as "color of skin." He learned that she had been born in Georgia in December 1862, that she could read and write, and that she had been married for 18 years. Then she spoke about her husband, James, also black, some twenty years her senior, and a traveling steelworker.

That's the encounter. Next comes some authorial commentary that contrasts what the participants think they know and what, in fact, is the truth. "Edward Brown took pride in the accuracy of his records, in the neat way in which he filled in the 1,350 blank boxes on each of his census sheets, recording into being a portrait of the polyglot neighborhood springing up in the sparsely settled borough of Queens. And so, he would have been stunned to learn that almost nothing Mrs. Todd told him was true."

Now the revelation, across two centuries, each false fact leading to a larger one, that sets up the fundamental irony that informs the book.

To begin with, she had knocked two years off her age, a gesture of vanity, perhaps. And she and her husband had been married for twelve years, not eighteen, a fact of which Mrs. Todd was surely aware, and a lie that seems hard to fathom, since the children's ages raised no questions about their legitimacy. But the other untruths were more stunning. Her husband was not black. He was not from the West Indies. He was not a steelworker. Even his name, James Todd, was a lie. Ada Todd was in fact married to Clarence King, an acclaimed public figure and the person Secretary of State John Hay once called "the best and brightest man of his generation."

King was a larger-than-life character: an explorer of the American West, a geologist, an accomplished writer and storyteller. He hobnobbed with presidents and congressmen and counted some of the nation's most distinguished writers and artists among his closest friends. His physical agility and bravery, combined with his keen intellect and wit, commanded near reverence from those who knew him best. With King, the historian Henry Adams wrote, "men worshiped not so much their friend, as the ideal American they all wanted to be." But of all this, of her husband's true identity and even his real name, Ada had not a clue.

Not until he lay dying of tuberculosis in late 1901, his last desperate hope of a desert cure gone, did James Todd write a letter to his wife telling her who he really was.[10]

The contrasts multiply, the ironies with them. In the end, "the story of Clarence and Ada King is about love and longing that transcend the historical bounds of time and place." Yet the "fissures of race and class that cut through the landscape of American life" prove as "deep and enduring" as the geologic rifts Clarence once explored. Those rifts are "even harder to explain," and so while the love story might transcend its place and time, it proves more difficult to transcend the irony with which their tale is told. Could Clarence's deathbed letter redeem his original deception? Can a coda relocate a narrative arc once it is anchored?[11]

Intellectual Settings

Stephen Greenblatt, *The Swerve*

Here is Stephen Greenblatt sketching the origins of Renaissance humanism, moving from a better way of designing script to "a project that linked the creation of something new with a search for something ancient . . . a shared mania, one whose origin can be traced back to Petrarch, who, a generation before Poggio's birth, had made the recovery of the cultural heritage of classical Rome a collective obsession."[12]

The myth of Petrarch as literary Promethean: it was a role exaggerated by acolytes and easily qualified by subsequent scholarship. But the source of the mythology itself is part of the story. In recreating a sense of what those early scholars did and the world in which they lived, Greenblatt reaches for analogies that help make tangible an intellectual journey. The landscape of ideas resembled the landscape of hills and ruins in which they lived their profane lives.

> But it is difficult entirely to demystify the movement to which Petrarch gave rise, if only because he and his contemporaries were so articulate about their experience. To them at least it did not seem obvious that the search on which they embarked was only a polite stroll onto well-trodden ground. They saw themselves as adventurous explorers both in the physical world—the mountains they crossed, the monastic libraries they investigated, the ruins they dug up—and in their inner world of desire. The urgency of the enterprise reflects their underlying recognition that there was nothing obvious or inevitable about the attempt to recover or imitate the language, material objects, and cultural achievements of the very distant past. It was a strange thing to do, far stranger than continuing to live the ordinary, familiar life that men and women had lived for centuries, making themselves more or less comfortable in the midst of the crumbling, mute remains of antiquity.

That is the movement's project. Its consequences follow:

Those remains were everywhere visible in Italy and throughout Europe: bridges and roads still in use after more than a millennium, the broken walls and arches of ruined baths and markets, temple columns incorporated into churches, old inscribed stones used as building materials in new constructions, fractured statues and broken vases. But the great civilization that left these traces had been destroyed. The remnants could serve as walls to incorporate new houses, as reminders that all things pass and are forgotten, as mute testimony to the triumph of Christianity over paganism, as literal quarries to be mined for precious stones and metals. Generations of men and women, in Italy and elsewhere in Europe, had developed effective techniques for the recycling of classical fragments, in their writing as well as their building. The techniques bypassed any anxiety about meddling with the leftover of a pagan culture: as broken shards whether of stone or of language, the leftovers were at once useful and unthreatening. What more would anyone want with the rubble over which the living had clambered for more than a thousand years?

To insist on the original, independent meaning of this rubble would cause trouble and moral perplexity.[13]

In this way Petrarch and his fellow travelers made a new world out of the past. But that task is not so different from the charge today to assemble the fragments of the past into forms acceptable to modern scholarship and then give them expression. We no longer look to Cicero or Livy for exemplars. We don't aspire to emulate their style. We struggle instead to enter the moral universe they inhabited. Yet in appealing to the basics of rhetoric and composition, in looking for tropes that can express tricky concepts in vernacular language, and in relying on form to help bear the weight of arguments, we may share more than we recognize. Our texts are full of literary fragments from the past.

Interlude

Every Day's a Burn Day

Ask fire officers in the Southeast how they manage to get so much controlled burning done and everywhere you will hear the same refrain: Every day's a burn day.

The default setting is to burn. You assume you will burn unless something out of your control stops you. You don't hold off until the weather and fuel align ideally. You don't wait for all the scientific studies to come in. You don't let minor irritants stall the program. You come to work expecting to burn, and if you are not in the field, you are readying equipment, tweaking burn plans, requesting spot weather forecasts, or preparing sites. You learn by doing. Burn day after day, and the acres add up. The Apalachicola National Forest and Eglin Air Force Base each burn about 100,000 acres a year, or an average of 275 acres a day. Do that year after year and each successive burn becomes easier. A prescribed fire is not an exceptional event: it's what you do.

A few years ago I created a graduate course on nonfiction writing. Many of the students who enroll are talented, and all want to write. Yet most struggle to get it done. They take the course for training and counsel, and to understand why they don't accomplish what they seek. They want to glean the right techniques, the insider strategies, the tricks of the trade that allow high-volume writers to meet their expanding deadlines. I tell them it's not about when you write or how you mentally gear up each day or what kind of notebook you carry in your pocket or purse. It's an attitude that is also a commitment. Every day's a writing day.

You will write until something stops you. You won't wait until mood and theme decide to sit by each other. You won't put off outlines and test pages until all the formal research is in because the actual writing will determine where the research goes. You won't let errands, emails, and elective tasks deflect you. You write, or you do stuff that leads to writing. Write day after day and the pages add up. Write a page a day and you could publish a book a year. A writing course can give you some experience, particularly in self-editing, which can translate into a hardier self-confidence and maybe a stiffer self-determination. But the only way to learn to write is to write.

Most people who want to write have a few essays or a book in them, just as most fire folks do a few burns or fight a big wildfire or two in that time of their life known as fire season. But those who do it as a career or a way of life do it every day because every day's a burn day.

3

Words on Words

In which we consider not only the texts of the historic record but those texts made from them.

I n his *Elements of Eloquence* Mark Forsyth demonstrates how William Shakespeare, with the use of alliteration, transformed Thomas North's 1579 translation of Plutarch's *Lives of the Noble Greeks and Romans* into blank verse:

We know this is the version Shakespeare used because you can sometimes see him using the same word that North used, and sometimes pairs of words. But when Shakespeare got to the big speech of the whole play, when he really needed some poetry, when he wanted true greatness, when he wanted to describe the moment that Antony saw Cleopatra on the barge and fell in love with her—he just found the relevant paragraph in North and copied it out almost word for word. *Almost* word for word.

Here's North:

. . . she disdained to set forward otherwise but to take her barge in the river Cydnus, the poop whereof was of gold, the sails of purple, and the oars of silver, which kept stroke in rowing after

the sound of the music of flutes, howboys, cithernes, viols, and
such other instruments as they played on the barge.

And here's Shakespeare:

The barge she sat in like a burnished throne,
Burned on the water: the poop was beaten gold:
Purple the sails and so perfumed that
The winds were lovesick with them; the oars were silver,
Which to the tune of flutes kept stroke, and made
The water which they beat to follow faster,
As amorous of their strokes.

The passage, as Forsythe notes, is "definitely half stolen." But the Bard changed its tempo, introduced alliteration, and transformed mundane description into evocative poetry.[1]

In less flamboyant ways that is what literary nonfiction can do to the words of history. You aren't allowed to change quoted words, but you can certainly rewrite them in ways that remain true to the facts and set them into a context that illuminates their meaning. For some historians the discovery and reproduction of the original words is enough. For most, and certainly for audiences who are not professionally obsessed, they need to be recast into the language of the times and, if it can be done without distorting the text beyond its meaning, into a context that adds to its significance.

A palimpsest is a document in which texts are written over previous, half-erased texts. This no longer happens literally on parchment or velum but it does occur figuratively as historians—or historical commentators— write and rewrite from the same sources but adapt them to their own times. The samples that follow show how writers have interacted with the preserved record to make something new. Our interest lies not with the resulting texts as historiography but as literature; not in the arguments or themes they advance but with the craft of arguing and evoking.

The selections themselves follow a rough chronology, with the oldest first. The primary purpose of each selection is to illustrate some aspect of literary craft, not to hold forth on historiography or the changing mores of an increasingly professional guild or the metaphysical wobbles of narrative. But their sequence does represent, very loosely, in an incidental way, an evolution of styles among historians, or writers looking to history for a subject, seeking to write for a general audience in their own times.

Edward Gibbon, *The Decline and Fall of the Roman Empire* (1788)

We shouldn't ignore Gibbon, whose multivolume opus remains the geodetic marker for historical scholarship since the Enlightenment. But he is hardly a model. His polished prose is archaic, if sonorous. He writes like Cicero might have spoken. His long sentences and paragraphs, while integrative, require close reading. As befits someone immersed in classical Roman history, his diction is richer in Latinate words than in Anglo-Saxon. His prose, however polished, feels artificial, less resonant than the boisterous English of the Elizabethan age that preceded the neoclassical Augustan.

Yet there are lessons in the prose, particularly in its use of parallelism, its ability to compact and integrate much information, and its use of comparisons to sharpen profiles and judgments. It's hard not to read a passage like the following and not wish to find a way to do the same:

> The various modes of worship, which prevailed in the Roman world, were all considered by the people, as equally true; by the philosopher, as equally false; and by the magistrate, as equally useful. And thus toleration produced not only mutual indulgence, but even religious concord.[2]

Or consider the value of rhetoric in holding together a fistful of observations about the status of Britain during the early Empire.

> The only accession which the Roman empire received, during the first century of the Christian era, was the province of Britain. In this single instance the successors of Caesar and Augustus were persuaded to follow the example of the former, rather than the precept of the latter. The proximity of its situation to the coast of Gaul seemed to invite their arms; the pleasing, though doubtful intelligence, of a pearl fishery, attracted their avarice; and as Britain was viewed in the light of a distinct and insulted world, the conquest scarcely formed any exception of the general system of continental measures. After a war of about forty years, undertaken by the most stupid, maintained by the most dissolute, and terminated by the most timid of all the emperors, the far greater part of the island submitted to the Roman yoke.[3]

Today we might translate that passage into something like this:

> The one exception to the observation that Rome's imperial borders were fixed was Britain. The empire followed the example of Julius Caesar, who started the conquest, rather than listen to Augustus, who had misgivings. The isle tempted. It was close to Gaul. It was rumored to have a pearl fishery. It didn't upset the empire elsewhere. Victory looked easy, safe, and cheap. The conquest, as far north as it got, took forty years. A dumb emperor waged the war. A wastrel emperor kept it going. A timid emperor ended it.

Note that the general structure of the passage remains—there is little reason to alter it. The parallelism persists, too—it's too useful to dump. What has changed is the voice, even more intolerant (to the extent possible); the diction, with direct English words rather than Latinate ones; and the breakup of long sentences (and paragraphs) into shorter ones. One marker of the difference is the loss of careful transitions, both in sentence construction and punctuation. The long, integrative passages are gone. So are the semicolons. What is also lost are intangibles like the texture of a voice that surely results in part from Gibbon's encounter with the dense array of sources that marinated his understanding. The rewriter only has Gibbon's text, not the press of materials it distilled. What remains in the rewrite is Gibbon's judgment, his sense that this was, to put it politely, a misplaced undertaking. In Gibbon's magisterial prose there is a sense of the epic. In the rewrite there is a hint of the satirical, if not the snarky.

Why would anyone read Edward Gibbon today? The scholarship has advanced immensely, not only in the number of sources but in their variety. Gibbon's narrative is, by today's standards, flawed, full of lapses and improper emphases. He saw Rome through the prism of his times, not ours. Surely, he belongs as a footnote to historiography, not as a literary model. We admire Shakespeare's prose, but we don't study his plays in order to write history as *Hamlet* or biography as *King Lear*.

In his *Autobiography*, Gibbon suggests why. After completing his final manuscript, he contemplated the life he had yet to live without the consuming labors of the *History*. "But my pride was soon humbled, and a sober melancholy was spread over my mind . . . whatsoever may be the future fate of the *History*, the life of the historian must be short and precarious." Art can outlive the artist. The reason to read Gibbon today is to appreciate his wit, his aesthetic sensibility, and his moral temper. We read him for the same reason we might read his contemporary novelists or philosophers, for the way in which writing conveyed his world. We read him not as a historian. We read him as a writer.[4]

That's the continuing reason to read some Gibbon. And it's the reason to write like the Gibbon of your day.

Francis Parkman, *Montcalm and Wolfe* (1885)

The prestige of the monarchy was declining with the ideas that had given it life and strength. A growing disrespect for king, ministry, and clergy was beginning to prepare the catastrophe that was still some forty years in the future. While the valleys and low places of the kingdom with dark nights were bright with fastidious, witty,—craving the pleasures of the mind as well as of the senses, criticizing everything, analyzing everything, believing nothing. Voltaire was in the midst of it, hating, with all his vehement soul, the abuses that swarmed about him, and assailing them with the inexhaustible shafts of his restless and piercing intellect. Montesquieu was showing to a despot-ridden age the principles of political freedom. Diderot and D'Alembert were beginning their revolutionary Encyclopaedia. Rousseau was sounding the first notes of his mad eloquence,—the wild revolt of a passionate and diseased genius against a world of falsities and wrongs. The *salons* of Paris, cloyed with other pleasures, alive to all that was racy and new, welcomed the pungent doctrines, and played with them as children play with fire, thinking no danger; as time went on, even embraced them in a genuine spirit of hope and good-will for humanity. The Revolution began at the top,—in the world of fashion, birth, and intellect,—and propagated itself downwards. "We walked on a carpet of flowers," Count Ségur afterwards said, "unconscious that it covered an abyss," till the gulf yawned at least, and swallowed them.[5]

It's a famously majestic prose, full of parallelism and vibrant adjectives, and of sharp judgments, lofted by an elevated tone that befits the epic saga of two empires contesting for the future of North America, beginning with the perspective of an omniscient observer and concluding with the lament of a single person. Yet the language by itself is not sufficient. Such prose would seem pompous in historical fiction; and if Parkman were spouting nonsense, the sonorous rhythms would ring hollow and read ridiculous.

Times change, tastes change; the records of the era accumulate, the moral universe within which history is recorded evolves. The judgments of historians and the means of expressing them must shift along with them. Some 140 years after *Montcalm and Wolfe* was published, no one reads Parkman for his monumental researches. As with Gibbon they read him for his art; the more committed, for his craft; the more philosophical, for his moral sense. We read him less for what he says about eighteenth-century France and England than for what he says about Gilded Age America. The biography of Louis XV matters less than the biography of his chronicler. We read Parkman as we would Herman Melville or Stephen Crane, as a cipher of his own time, who found in history a subject to animate him and in a Romantic prose a medium to express it. We read him to learn how to write history in the language of our times.

Harold Lamb, *The Crusades: Iron Men and Saints* (1930)

Mostly, Lamb hews close to the chronicles, and even quotes extensively with lengthy block quotes. Still, those accounts need context in terms of their geography and culture, and the personalities of their scribes. A string of passages, arranged like beads on a rosary, would make poor fare for most readers. So periodically Lamb breaks the text, often at the start of a new chapter, with the evocation of a scene full of sensory details, as with the following, which helps introduce the arrival of Bohemund:

> Spring had come to the Bosphorus. Judas tree blossoms gleamed in the dark foliage of wild vines. Streams whispered down the banks, under nodding aspens. The blue-green water lapped, in gently, tideless motion, against the stained granite pleasure palaces. These had been closed during the brief winter. Now the owners were flocking back in bright-cushioned caïques, rowed by slaves.
>
> Pennants fluttered from the long hunks of the imperial galleys moored against the bank. A courier's boat, oars swinging in unison, dashed by on its way to the guard-castle of Hieron. Fishermen in blunt barks made haste to get their nets out of the way.

As with the season, so it is with the day:

> The whispers dwindled and ceased, and the youthful patricians trooped off to go to the candle lighting at the Sancta Sophia. Behind the towers of the Golden Gate the sun had set. Lights gleamed from the embrasures of the high monasteries. Armed servitors tramped through the shadows. The sails of the fishing fleet moved in toward the shore.
>
> Dusk hid the Bosphorus. Colored lanterns bobbed in the bows of the caïques. Byzantium was setting out upon the business of the night. Byzantium, with its whispers and fears, was amusing itself as it had done for a thousand years. Pigeons fluttered slowly into the Judas trees, and the warm air became tranquil, redolent of damp grass and cookery.
>
> Only, from the snow peaks of Asia across the water, came a chill breath, sharp and ominous.[6]

Where do these details come from? Not from the chronicles themselves. They come from personal travel and background reading. They are facts, though not quotations, with a touch of personification ("Byzantium, with its whispers and fears . . ."). They do not pervert or deflect the narrative; there is no reason to believe they are invented solely from fancy or a desire to promote rhetorical sleights of hand. But they do advance a literary intention, or rather two.

The break pauses the story. The Crusade did not advance relentlessly but moved in lurches, stalls, and false starts. The scene setting allows the reader to regroup. Equally, the sensuous particulars, especially the languor and nuance they evoke, serve another purpose: they stand in stark contrast to the iron men, the knights, and to the iron purpose, the conquest of Jerusalem, that power the First Crusade. Though serious, the Byzantines amuse themselves, the Crusaders push on. The Byzantines scheme, the Crusaders fight. The long-settled city and its quotidian rituals act as a foil to the wandering horde of crusaders. The contrast suggests it will be hard to reconcile both groups to a common cause, and that proves the case.

So by drawing back from a close reading of the chronicles, Lamb allows the reader some breathing room, a chance to regroup at Byzantium (as the Crusaders did), and by carefully chosen description, he also sets up a contrast that will end in conflict.

Richard Lillard, *Desert Challenge: An Interpretation of Nevada* (1942)

Nevada, particularly early-America Nevada, seems to invite evocative prose. Postwar Nevada, led by the explosive growth of Las Vegas, inspires more edge and glitter. The early era spoke to loss and decay, the newer, to booms based on metal in coins rather than in hard-rock ore. In the first, Nevada is dead—littered with dead playas, dead mountains, dead towns. Here is Richard Lillard's description of the boomtowns that went bust.

> Nevada had hardly become a state when already it was strewn with dead towns where temporarily the course of empire had taken its way. Inevitably even the most flourishing mining camps reached their peak of production and began a decline. Cables and ore cars grew rusty. Sage brush and shad scale crept over the dumps. The householder filled his traveling bags and his Saratoga trunk, pulled down the shades, and left behind him a furnished home. The merchant either gutted his store or cast an appraising eye on the shelves of goods and simply locked the door. The colored bottles in the drugstore window gleamed dimly through cobwebs. A big wooden boot dangled from a decaying awning to announce a shoemaker who no longer plied awl and hammer. The potted geranium in the restaurant window withered into a gaunt stalk, and the vase of wandering Jew dried into a curved yellow furl and blew down on the warping floor. Two-story business blocks stood useless in the bleaching sun.[7]

This generic scene is made vivid by the details—the boot, the geranium, the Saratoga trunk. Instead of an abstract statement (bust followed boom), appealing only to the mind, the scene becomes manifest to the senses. But it needs some empirical details, too, which come by way of examples.

> Towns often died with dramatic speed between one census and another. Hamilton fell from 8,000 in 1869 to about 100 ten years later; Treasure City, from 6,000 to 50. In less than a decade Shermantown went from 7,000 to one family and Swansea from 3,000 to none. Belmont produced some $15,000,000 worth of silver and lead between 1865 and 1885 and then collapsed. A smokestack stood on, 175 feet high, made of bricks hauled by ox teams the five hundred miles from Sacramento. Washoe City had 1,500 in the early sixties, when it was a complete community, with churches, schools, and sawmills. It was down to 70 by 1875. Thereafter it declined more slowly, until in 1919 there was one inhabitant, a saloon-keeper along the highway. The Nevada prohibition law of that year put him out of business. Reveille, in Nye County, was once a busy town of 400 persons. Its life ebbed when the price of lead fell after the Armistice, and its last citizen froze to death in his cabin during zero weather in 1923.
>
> Eureka produced $50,000,000 in lead and sliver between 1873 and 1896. At one time it was second only to the Comstock in production, but finally the mines struck more water than could profitably be pumped. The Richmond Refinery closed, leaving a dump of 700,000 tons of ore. The Eureka Consolidated closed, and most of the eight thousand inhabitants took the stage or the narrow-gauge railroad that connected with the Southern Pacific at Palisade. No longer were there five fire companies, two militias, a brass band, and a busy Opera House. Spent was the glory of the Eureka Hook and Ladder Company and the Knickerbocker Hose Company. Only the nine graveyards were as populous as ever, with simple pine slabs being added to mark the deaths of old men. A "wise guy" from Salt Lake City remarked that the town had enough graveyards to bury decently everything that ever died there, with the single exception of the town itself.

As economic and social life departed, buildings and improvements did likewise. Floods and cloudbursts gouged foundations, floated off outbuildings, and smashed in walls. Fire turned whole blocks into charcoal. With the coming of the automobile age, looters and wreckers rode in. They ripped up the board sidewalks and saloon floors and panned the dirt for lost coins and spilled gold dust. In Aurora this netted several hundred dollars. Under the floor of an assay office lay $2,500 waiting to be panned. The thick concrete that floored an old mill was worth $15 a ton because of the gold-bearing chemicals that had permeated it. Prowlers searched the walls and fireplaces of cabins, hoping to find a secret cache of money or metal. Legitimately or illegitimately there were valuable finds for souvenir hunters. The Henry Ford of Greenfield Village sent an agent to collect old newspapers. He pulled some from cabin walls, where they had served as wallpaper. W. Parker Lyon, retired warehouse operator in Los Angeles, acquired hundreds of thousands of relics for his Pony Express Museum: gold-dust scales, Wells, Fargo ledgers, nickelodeons, joss-house ornaments, ladies' clothes, hand-drawn fire engines, barber chairs, and so on.[8]

A clear topic sentence organizes the details, and the mechanical repetition of declarative sentences seems to emulate the mechanical life-cycling of the towns as they erode into the urban slag heaps left by industrial mining. Rather than simply state that Nevada towns went boom and bust, Lillard shows it. The passage not only advances a thesis but makes it memorable. The towns come and go like the flashfloods that fill a playa and then dry into salt.

Wallace Stegner, *Beyond the Hundredth Meridian* (1953)

If Harold Lamb's evocation of Byzantium could also serve as an exemplary description of a place and Richard Lillard's of a historical process, Wallace Stegner's sketch of Big Bill Stewart could work as a character profile of a person. For our purposes, the interest lies in Stegner's trade-mark fusion of colloquial language with formal rhetoric. As William Shakespeare rewrote known stories and biographies but with a flourish that made them memorable and invested them with more meaning, so Stegner uses literary tropes to recreate portraits.

> Robust, aggressive, contentious, narrow, self-made, impatient of "the-orists," irritated by abstract principles, a Nevada lawyer, miner, Indian-killer; a fixer, a getter-done, an indefatigable manipulator around the whisky and cigars, a dragon whose cave was the smoke-filled room, Big Bill Stewart was one to delight a caricaturist and depress a patriot. But he was also, in his way, a man of faith: he believed in Western "development," and he believed in the right of men—himself among them—to get rich by this "development." He was a man of a hard, driving strength, a formi-dable partisan. The water that was the life to his state, both for agriculture and for mining, had to come from the mountains, and to bring it from the mountains meant dams and ditches. Before he ever took up the law or entered politics, Stewart had built ditches and brought water to min-ing camps, and he thought he knew how it should be done. Now that sites for reservoirs were being picked off and water appropriated at the heads of the streams, some of Stewart's constituents down below were beginning to suffer, and the possibilities of settlement in the valleys, the hope of new voters and new votes and new powers, were threatened. It was primarily to promote water development in Nevada that Stewart had been returned to Washington. He was not one to hesitate before dif-ficulties or to look past acts toward consequences. Ask for a half million the first year, he kept telling Powell. Get after it. Get it done.[9]

Wallace Stegner thought of himself primarily as a novelist, and taught creative writing, but some of his most memorable prose came when he applied that sensibility to nonfiction, when he played against grain and character. In a similar manner his resort to near-slangy language and his use of classical rhetorical devices would seem contrived and dated by themselves but joined produce a fizz, like otherwise inert sodium bicarbonate and water when stirred together. A quick, final example, unsurprisingly focused on a character.

> Poor Sam Adams was doomed never to reap the rewards, whether for patents or exploration. He was a preposterous, twelve-gauge, hundred-proof, kiln-dried, officially notarized fool, or else he was one of the most wildly incompetent scoundrels who ever lived.[10]

Most writing manuals urge authors to treat adjectives as literary leaches; the more that are removed, the healthier the text. But Stegner deliberately defies that dictum: he piles adjective upon adjective. If he had stopped at two or three, the effect would seem merely wordy. But his exuberance of everyday, slangy derogatories works because it is clear that Stegner intends excess, and that Adams is himself an expression of folk excess. If you are going against the grain of convention, do it whole-heartedly and with a wink at the reader.

Barbara W. Tuchman, *The Proud Tower: A Portrait of the World Before the War, 1890–1914* (1965)

The book's details are wonderful, but its frame is what holds the mosaic together. Moreover, for such an extraordinary event as the prelude to the Great War, it would be easy to anticipate giddily, to overshadow the foreshadows, and to hyperventilate into exhaustion. Instead, we find a touch of parallelism, a sly analogy, a deft touching on topics, and a sparkling closing quote suffice to lift the prose from the plodding but not so high it becomes untethered.

> The diplomatic origins, so-called, of the Great War are only the fever chart of the patient; they do not tell us what caused the fever. To probe for underlying causes and deeper forces one must operate within the

framework of a whole society and try to discover what moved the people in it. I have tried to concentrate on society rather than the state. Power politics and economic rivalries, however important, are not my subject.

The period of this book was above all the culmination of a century of the most accelerated rate of change in man's record. Since the last explosion of a generalized belligerent will in the Napoleonic wars, the industrial and scientific revolutions had transformed the world. Man had entered the Nineteenth Century using only his own and animal power, supplemented by that of wind and water, much as he had entered the Thirteenth, or, for that matter, the First. He entered the Twentieth with his capacities in transportation, communication, production, manufacture and weaponry multiplied a thousandfold by the energy of machines. Industrial society gave man new powers and new scope while at the same time building up new pressures in prosperity and poverty, in growth of population and crowding in cities, in antagonisms of classes and groups, in separation from nature and from satisfaction in individual work. Science gave man new welfare and new horizons while it took away belief in God and certainty in a scheme of things he knew. By the time he left the Nineteenth Century he had as much new unease as ease. Although *fin de siècle* usually connotes decadence, in fact society at the turn of the century was not so much decaying as bursting with new tensions and accumulated energies. Stefan Zweig who was thirty-three in 1914 believed that the outbreak of war "had nothing to do with ideas and hardly even with frontiers. I cannot explain it otherwise than by this surplus force, a tragic consequence of the internal dynamism that had accumulated in forty years of peace and now sought violent release."[11]

So much for the tea-cup rim of the war. Its bitter dregs match these rhythms, but with less energy, and another concluding quote contrasts the enthusiasms that began the drama with the empty catharsis that concludes it.

The proud tower built up through the great age of European civilization was an edifice of grandeur and passion, of riches and beauty and dark cellars. Its inhabitants lived, as compared to a later time, with more self-reliance, more confidence, more hope; greater magnificence, extravagance and elegance; more careless ease, more gaiety, more pleasure in each other's company and conversation, more injustice and hypocrisy, more misery and want, more sentiment including false sentiment, less sufferance of mediocrity, more dignity in work, more delight in nature, more zest. The Old World had much that has since been lost, whatever may have been gained. Looking back on it from 1915 Emile Verhaeren, the Belgian Socialist poet, dedicated his pages, "With emotion, to the man I used to be."[12]

The book is a study in contrasts, not only within each society, or among the separate nations, but between generations, and in the end between days of a single life, and it needs a vehicle to transport those contrasts. Not inflated vocabulary (or elevated jargon), nor rhetorical tricks, but powerful ideas and a robust sensibility carry the day. The literary skill allows them to speak simply and not trip over one another.

David McCulloch, *The Path Between the Seas: The Creation of the Panama Canal, 1870–1914* (1978)

The book is chocked with fine portraits of the principals—Ferdinand de Lesseps, Theodore Roosevelt, Philippe Bunau-Varilla, John Stevens, G. W. Goethals, among many others; but the "special wonder" of the Panama Canal was the great dig through the Cordillera. Nothing else so captured the imagination, so let David McCulloch describe the famed Culebra Cut.

It was the great focus of attention, regardless of whatever else was happening at Panama. The building of Gatun Dam or the construction of the locks, projects of colossal scale and expense, were always of secondary interest so long as the battle raged in that nine-mile stretch between Bas Obispo and Pedro Miguel. The struggle lasted seven years, from 1907 through 1913, when the rest of the world was still at peace, and in the dry seasons, the tourists came by the hundreds, by the thousands as time went on, to stand and watch from grassy vantage points hundreds of feet above it all. Special trains had to be arranged to bring them out from Colón and Panama City, tour guides provided, and they looked no different from the Sunday crowds on the Boardwalk at Atlantic City. Gentlemen wore white shoes and pale straw hats; ladies stepped along over the grass in ankle-length skirts and carried small, white umbrellas as protection from the sun. A few were celebrities: Alice Roosevelt Longworth, Lord Bryce, President Taft, and William Jennings Bryan (who "evinced more general excitement than anyone since T.R."). "He who did not see the Culebra Cut during the mighty work of excavation," declared an author of the day, "missed one of the great spectacles of the ages—a sight that no other time, or place was, or will be, given to man to see." Lord Bryce called it the greatest liberty ever taken with nature.[13]

The special problem with the Cut was the landslides that routinely slushed down and filled up the excavation. The only solution was to landscape on a scale sufficient to allow a new angle of repose: instead of a canal-like cut, the project would have to dig a valley with dimensions suitable to Panama's regimen of rock and rain. Then "on January 19 Cucaracha broke loose once again. It was one of the worst slides on record. It spilled the whole way across the Cut and up the other side. All traffic was blocked at that end; for the sixth or seventh time, the slide had wiped out months of work."

Gaillard was practically in shock, according to one account, and Goethals was hurriedly called to the scene. "What are we to do now?" Gaillard asked. Goethals lit a cigarette. "Hell," he said, "dig it out again."[14]

The sentiment is almost expected—could be in lesser hands a cliché. What makes it memorable is the right detail, in this case, the cigarette. *The Path Between the Seas* does not make the Culebra Mountains the focus, as an environmental historian might. The Cut (as with the Canal generally) is refracted through its effect on people—on tourists, on American society, on the men responsible for digging and hauling. Note, again, the use of a choice paragraph- and chapter-ending quote.

The book appeared at a time of growing divorce between professional and popular historians—the former suspicious of big narratives, the latter dependent on them. It was also a time in which those interested in nonfiction but with literary ambitions sidestepped into New Journalism, leaving academic history with those who wanted to make it a social science. What resulted was a weakening of classic rhetoric; a softening of diction into more colloquial language; a slackening of formal structure into the rhythms of more vernacular storytelling.

While it's hard to segregate individual temperament from that of the times, making it difficult to extrapolate from McCulloch's style to prevailing taste, it seems that the bond between high prose and grand topics was loosening. The people without history were about to meet the prose without rhetoric.

David Quammen, *Spillover: Animal Infections and the Next Human Pandemic* (2013)

David Quammen is generally regarded as a gifted writer of popular science. But when you deal with such topics as Charles Darwin, evolution, the biogeography of extinction, and convey information by telling stories, you are in fact if not title doing history. What happens, however, when the needs of narrative as a form clash with the documentation? When the evidence is too sparse, too contradictory, or too confused? When narrative as a way of sorting through the clutter is unavailable because it requires a level of chronological detail and agency that doesn't exist? In such circumstances, the rules are clear and unyielding: you color within the lines. You don't make things up and pass them off as the right stuff.

There are alternative strategies, however. It's possible to lighten or even elide transitions without falsifying. It's acceptable to make the author's quest for the story into itself the organizing story. And its possible to draw other lines so long as you explain unequivocally to the reader what you are doing. In his chapter on AIDS for *Spillover*, Quammen shows such a strategy at work.

He notes that research has identified the likely place and time for the first human infection: southeastern Cameroon no later than 1908. What Quammen needs is an agent to receive the virus and then spread it; the person becomes a protagonist and the propagation of the virus, a plot. There is no way, however, to identify how the AIDS virus leaped from chimpanzee to human or who was the first, but it is possible to imagine several scenarios. Quammen is partial to the idea that a hunter of bush meat was cut while butchering a chimp and that blood passed between them. He conjures up a scene, and what matters is that he says explicitly that he is imagining the scene. He doesn't recreate it and pretend it happened. His account is a possibility, no more—a literary and historical hypothesis—but one that allows him to infuse the moment with vivid details.

Let's give him due stature: not just a cut hunter but the Cut Hunter. Assuming he lived thereabouts in the first decade of the twentieth century, he probably captured his chimpanzee with a snare made from a forest vine, or in some other form of trap, then killed the animal with a spear. He may have been a Baka man, living independently with his extended family in the forest or functioning as a sort of serf under the "protection" of a Bantu village chief. But probably he wasn't, given what I'd heard of Baka scruples about eating ape. More likely he was Bantu, possibly of the Mpiemu or the Kako or one of the other ethnic groups inhabiting the upper Sangha River basin. Or he may have been a

Bakwele, involved in the practice of beka. There's no way of establishing his identity, or even his ethnicity, but this remote southeastern corner of what was then Germany's Kamerun colony offered plenty of candidates. I imagine the man thrilled and a bit terrified when he found a chimpanzee caught in his snare. He had proved himself a successful hunter, a provider, a proficient member of his little community—and he wasn't yet cut.

The chimp too, tethered by a foot or a hand, would have been terrified as the man approached, but also angry and strong and dangerous. Maybe the man killed it without getting hurt; if so, he was lucky. Maybe there was an ugly fight; he might even have been pummeled by the chimp, or badly bitten. But he won. Then he would have butchered his prey, probably on the spot (discarding the entrails but not the organs, such as heart and liver, which were much valued) and probably with a machete or an iron knife. At some point during the process, perhaps as he struggled to hack through the chimp's sternum or disarticulate an arm from its socket, the man injured himself.

I imagine him opening a long, sudden slice across the back of his left hand, into the muscular web between thumb and forefinger, his flesh smiling out pink and raw almost before he saw the damage or felt it, because his blade was so sharp. And then immediately his wound bled. By a lag of some seconds, it also hurt. The Cut Hunter kept working. He'd been cut before and it was an annoyance that barely dimmed his excitement over the prize. His blood flowed out and mingled with the chimp's, the chimp's flowed in and mingled with his, so that he couldn't quite tell which was which. He was up to his elbows in gore. He wiped his hand. Blood leaked again into his cut, dribbled again into it from the chimp, and again he wiped. He had no way of knowing—no language or words or thoughts by which to conceive—that this animal was SIV-positive. The idea didn't exist in 1908.[15]

The passage is full of vivid details, all plausible but none confirmed. Its inquiry might well have proceeded along the terms of a thesis: the first infection might have happened among these peoples, all of whom for one reason or another could have been at this place at this time and doing stuff that might have allowed for infection. Each proposal could then be met, paragraph by paragraph, with evidence for and against. It would be done well—someone with Isaiah Berlin's skills could probably make it compelling. But Quammen has chosen a more broadly accessible form, the story, so he needs a character, a scene, and a conflict, and gets them.

The saga unfolds. The Cut Hunter infects his wife, dies during an elephant hunt, and the widow finds another man, a trader ("also hypothetical but fitted to the facts"), whom she infects. Quammen calls him the Voyager. He is another fictitious character—overtly identified as such—who carries the tale to the point where the documentary record can pick up the narrative baton. "No one can know, not even in this imagined scenario," whether the plausible details are correct. The details, though they radiate conviction, remain hypothetical. His adopted form brings its own requirements—chronology demands a degree of continuity, the tale requires a character as agent, and with his storied re-creation Quammen supplies them. But because he is clear about what is imagined and what can be documented, all his local color remains within bounds.[16]

These samples of historical writing have unfolded as a chronicle, not a narrative. No theme joins them. They were selected because they illustrate some element of literary craft. But they are also works that managed to meld some standards of scholarship with readability that made them popular among a literate public. What trends might we see?

They are the same shifts we find in comparing the literature of the periods in which they were written. There is less rhetorical scaffolding—less willingness to openly imitate classic style—which probably reflects less training in rhetoric and the classics. The scaffoldings are hidden. There is more everyday language and more colloquial construction. Normal speech, elevated, not formal exemplars, emulated, is the foundation.

Passages are shorter, and less likely to be joined into long constructions. Chapters, too, tend to be shorter, or even abolished in favor of sequences of sketches. This shift segues into another: transitions are more abrupt, or dropped. If we were to widen our selections to include commentaries, we would likely find even less formal language, with structure resembling the rhetorical equivalent of slang, and attitude replacing literary voice. In a time when information has become a commodity, when googling replaces research, the relation between form and fluidity is bound to change. Style conveys interpretation more than information.

What is worth exploring are those texts that manage to fuse the formal with the colloquial. They don't abandon standards of scholarship or violate the rules of nonfiction, yet they find ways to make texts readable by the tastes of the day. It's easy to flip to one polarity or the other: to insist that the sources must dictate the style, even if presenting them makes for sluggish reading; or to plead that the story, its readability, its flair, the sweetness of its closure, makes a different truth possible. In one, the data drives the style and belongs with academic writing. In the other, the style shapes the data and bleeds into fiction. Each has its justifications why the choice is the best or appears the only one possible.

But neither is literary nonfiction, the essence of which is to live in that zone of tension between those poles, the way a drop of oil can be suspended between oppositely charged plates. G. K. Chesterton once observed that the "Christian ideal" wasn't tried and found wanting but tried and found difficult, and so not really tried. With a genuflection to imitation and nod to modernizing, we might say the same about literary nonfiction.

4

The Poisonous Passive

In which we explore the fanatic (and misplaced) vituperation directed at the passive voice.

As a group, academics pay little attention to writing. It is enough if a text is grammatically correct and "readable." They don't teach it, as though student prose just blossoms like daffodils from bulbs. But on one matter there is near-universal agreement: the passive voice is evil. If an auto-correcting program existed to convert the passive into the active, as apps do typos, they would clamor for it. So, while most academic historians (to name names) are happy to "contest" or "subvert" nearly every narrative, and even narrative itself as a principle, they would likely lump any effort to defend the passive as the literary equivalent of Holocaust denial. No credible writer would willingly use the passive, and no credentialed historian would tolerate its defense.

Yet it's a curious obsession. The stock example of the evasive passive, one much beloved by critics, is the expression: "mistakes were made." Yet what better agency is conveyed by rewriting that fact into the active: "mistakes happened"? It does nothing to identify the agent of those mistakes. "Were made" suggests that they were made by someone. "Happened" suggests they just occurred, perhaps at the whims of Nature or Providence.

Steven Pinker (speaking of scientists, another group denounced for their reliance on the passive) notes that "if you follow the guideline, 'Change every passive sentence into an active sentence,' you don't improve the prose, because there's no way the passive construction could have survived in the English language for millennia if it hadn't served some purpose. It's an effective, and necessary workaround, for a language that relies on a rigid ordering of subject, verbs, and objects. The problem with any given construction, like the passive voice, isn't that people use it, but that they use it too much or in the wrong circumstances." So, too, the problem isn't the use of the passive in historical writing. It's the misuse of the passive by historians.[1]

Another critic of the critics, Geoffrey Pullum, notes that passive purists claim that using passives will make writing "weak, dull, vague, cowardly, bureaucratic, and dishonest," and argues in reply that "the specific stylistic charges leveled against the passive are entirely baseless." Many published critiques only reveal that the denouncers "cannot tell passives from actives," "confuse the grammatical concept with a rhetorical one involving inadequate attribution of agency or responsibility," and in general display "an extraordinary level of grammatical ignorance." The revulsion against the passive in fact emerged only in the twentieth century and became encoded in writing manuals such as William Strunk's *The Elements of Style* (1918).[2]

Pullum pursues his quarry into that guide's twenty-first-century edition:

The confused discussion is only amplified and worsened in the revisions made in later editions of *The Elements of Style* by E. B. White, where small changes to the examples are made. The most recent version of the books (Strunk and White 2000) contains the following tableau, where the sentences on the left are supposed to be bad, and the ones on the right are proposed as suitable corrections or replacements:

There were a great number of dead leaves lying on the ground.	Dead leaves covered the ground.
At dawn, the crowing of a rooster could be heard.	The cock's crow came with dawn.
The reason he left college was that his health became impaired.	Failing health compelled him to leave college.
It was not long before she was very sorry that she had said what she had.	She soon repented her words.

The original theme of replacing passive clauses by active transitives has now disappeared completely. The main difference between the examples in the two columns is that the favored ones on the right are significantly shorter than the allegedly bad ones. But there is not a single case in Strunk and White's tabular display of a passive in the left column corresponding to an active transitive on the right. In the second pair of examples, the right-hand version has an intransitive verb; and none of the others has a passive on the left (*impaired*, for example, is not a passive VP [verb phrase]—*become* cannot take passive clause complements, as we see from *Kennedy became shot by Oswald*).[3]

The issue is not the passive per se. The issue is lame, dull, confusing, belabored prose, and that is what is wrong with the knee-jerk criticism of the passive. There are, after all, plenty of occasions when the passive voice is misused (but the same can be said of the active). The problem is that it is unreflecting. It doesn't make writing conscious and highlight the choices a writer must make. To return to historians, history is about context, yet historical writing under such proscriptions removes verbs from their context of meaning, and meaning is the ultimate arbiter.

On the matter of context it probably helps understanding that William Strunk brought out his *Elements* when the United States was still immersed in the Progressive Era, a time of political ferment (and recently, of war), a time of doing in which the country also published its primary contribution to philosophy, Pragmatism. It was a time that preferred to act. The literature of the era is awash with gerunds.

One of its major political figures and writers, Gifford Pinchot, illustrates the Strunk prescriptions nicely. In 1907, while serving as the nation's chief forester, he issued his own handbook, this one for the proper management of the national forests. It was a slim volume, intended to fit into the pocket of a working ranger but also to explain to the public how the national forests would operate. Here is what it has to say on the critical subject of fire.

> The people have helped the Forest officers immensely in preventing and fighting fire. There are not half enough Rangers to suitably protect the Forests. The only way to keep fire down is for everyone to take a hand at it. Look out for small fires; they start big ones. See that camp fires are completely out before leaving them. Never burn brush or dangerous slashings in dry or windy weather. The time to fight fire is right at the start. When it once has a good headway it is often impossible to control it. As soon as fire is discovered put it out if you can, and in any case notify the nearest Forest officer at once and give him all the assistance possible.[4]

Such a passage could come straight out of Strunk's manual. It is not only driven by active verbs but by simple words (most of them Anglo-Saxon monosyllables). It would seem that such prose is exactly what a forty-two-page manual of operations should have.

Yet consider its introduction to the topic of the forests themselves, "How They Are Made"—the very title written in the passive.

> At first a great many of the National Forests were made without knowing exactly where the boundary lines should run. This was unfortunate; because some agricultural lands which should have been excluded were taken in, and a good deal of timber land was left out. This could have been avoided by making examinations on the ground, but there was no money for the work, and so the boundaries had to be drawn very roughly.[5]

Very few readers would find that passage unclear, but despite his taste for the active—in language as in life—Pinchot's text is full of passives. What accounts for the difference? In the first passage Pinchot is addressing fire, and the need for rangers and settlers to act on it. It has only one passive verb, but lots of imperatives. In the second passage, the subject is the character of the national forests, and this is something that was created, not something that could itself act. Pinchot might have made Congress or the president or the American public as his subject and described, with an active voice, what they did or didn't do or did poorly. Instead he is talking about the national forests and what happened to them, and so speaks in the passive. There is nothing garbled about the meaning or unsettled about agency.

Now fast-forward eighty-two years from *The Use Book* and seventy-two years from *The Elements of Style* and consider a text excised from Simon Schama's *Citizens*.

The battle itself had taken the lives of eighty-three of the citizens' army. Another fifteen were to die from wounds. Only one of the *invalides* had died in the fighting and three had been wounded. The imbalance was enough for the crowd to demand some sort of punitive sacrifice, and de Launay duly provided it. All of the hatred which to a large degree had been spared the garrison was concentrated on him. His attributes of command—a sword and baton—were wrenched away from him and he was marched towards the Hôtel de Ville through enormous crowds, all of whom were convinced he had been foiled in a diabolical plot to massacre the people. Hulin and Elie managed to prevent the crowd from killing him on the street, through more than once he was knocked down and badly beaten. Throughout the walk he was covered in abuse and spittle. Outside the Hôtel de Ville competing suggestions were offered as to how he should meet his end, including a proposal to tie him to a horse's tail and drag him over the cobbles. A pastry cook named Desnot said it would be better to take him into the Hôtel de Ville—but at that point de Launay, who had had enough of the ordeal, shouted "Let me die" and lashed out with his boots, landing a direct hit in Desnot's groin. He was instantaneously covered with darting knives, swords and bayonets, rolled to the gutter and finished off with a barrage of pistol shots.[6]

The evoked scene is vivid, the passage has plenty of action, there is no confusion over cause or agency, and the text is not encumbered with lumbering jargon or tangled syntax. Yet half its verbs are passives. Where de Launay acts, the voice is active. Where he is acted upon, the voice is passive. One could imagine all those nominally ugly passives rewritten into actives, but the effect would likely be to homogenize the text. The give and take of things done and done to would likely yield to a thudding sameness. There may be reasons to use such a style, if, say, the point is to emphasize the repetitious quality and universality of what happens, but that does not appear to be Schama's purpose. Rather, the rich prose captures something of the swirl of events. It's hard to imagine a reader suddenly stopped, amid this busy procession, by the intrusion of a de Launay–linked passive. Like the mob the prose surges on.

The fight over the passive voice is not just a phony war. It's a misplaced exercise in misdirection.

It simplifies good and bad writing into mechanical prescriptions (and proscriptions). You don't have to reconcile subject and style, or do the hard work of sieving through alternative constructions, or cultivate a voice, or write and rewrite a passage to temper the tone and smooth the flow and find the word with just the right connotations. You just have to wipe out the passive, as though editing a text were a game of space invaders, zapping away at every sinister appearance. Instead of framing a discussion about the passive as a question of context—how the verb sits within the text—it becomes a rote process of extirpation, like clearing a field of stumps. The passive can be—often is—misused. Deciding to use it should be a conscious choice. It can be the right one.

As a quick example, take a passage that will appear in a subsequent section of *Style and Story* on humor and nonfiction. Version one, in the active voice: "Humor makes stuff up, it leaves stuff out, it exaggerates up to and beyond the borders of nonfiction." Version two, in the passive: "Stuff is made up, stuff is left out, stuff is exaggerated up to and beyond the borders of nonfiction." Is there any confusion in either about agency or about what is happening? In the first sentence, humor is acting. In the second, stuff (the source material) is acted upon. Neither phrasing is intrinsically better grammatically. Which is better? As with so much of writing, it depends. A choice between them will lie with taste or subtle emphases. My own preference here is to accent what happens to the sources. Besides, the repeated use of "stuff" as subject seems, well, less stuffy.

In "Politics and the English Language," included in all anthologies of his work, George Orwell listed five "rules" that he believed would "cover most cases" of writing good English when "instinct fails." Rule four was "Never use the passive where you can use the active." Two sentences later he admits that a writer "could keep all" of these rules "and still write bad English." The opening sentence of the essay that follows in the *Collected Essays*, "Reflections on Gandhi," reads: "Saints should always be judged guilty until they are proved innocent, but the tests that have to be applied to them are not, of course, the same in all cases." Three passives in one sentence, and a lead sentence at that. No wonder Orwell's fifth rule was to "Break any of these rules sooner than say anything outright barbarous." Or in the case of his Gandhi essay, be forced to surrender a sentence's sense and its aesthetic appeal to rules. There is not the slightest murkiness in Orwell's Gandhi sentence. Or as Orwell stated repeatedly in various contexts, the particular matters more than the abstract.[7]

Interlude

The Imitative Fallacy

It would seem an axiom of design. A boring person should be boring. Chaos should be chaotic. A confusing scene should be, well, confusing. Writing should convey in its shape the sense of what it says in words. Anything else would violate the expected alignment of style with story.

Actually, no. The fact is, a passage about boredom should be interesting. A text about anarchy cannot be itself anarchic. A description of a confusing scene should convey or dramatize, as artfully as possible, the sense of confusion without itself becoming confusing. Design should support a theme, not simply emulate it.

To give the error a formal label call it the imitative fallacy, and it shows that not all design is equal. Unless you are experimenting with style—unless a style *is* the theme—it should advance the text, and it should be more or less invisible to the reader. It should do its work as unobtrusively as a car's engine. The point of a drive is not to highlight pistons: it's to move from place to place.

Great style does this invisibly. It provides extra thrust by greater efficiency, by having the text glide on its design. It does its job without itself becoming the labored point of the text. Almost any good text will illustrate the principle. But a fun demonstration is available in Mark Twain's *Life on the Mississippi*, in which, as a cub pilot, he learns how to read the river. Twain might have simply dumped everything a pilot needs to know onto the text to demonstrate the mountains of detail a pilot had to master—and he would likely have wrecked the text (along, no doubt, with the steamboat). The sum is overwhelming.

> "Now, if my ears hear aright, I have not only to get the names of all the towns and islands and bends, and so on, by heart, but I must even get up a warm personal acquaintanceship with every old snag and one-limbed cottonwood and obscure wood-pile that ornaments the banks of this river for twelve hundred miles; and more than that, I must actually know where these things are in the dark, unless these guests are gifted with eyes that can pierce through two miles of solid blackness. I wish the piloting business was in Jericho and I had never thought of it."[1]

Instead, the journey becomes a series of incremental lessons, each atop the others. Each tidbit added to the others, each reading finding a different texture. The reader learns as the cub pilot does, bend by bend, layer upon layer, but that learning is refracted through a persona, the re-created young Twain. The persona may be overwhelmed and confused, but the reader is not. Twain's authorial artifice comes by inventing an intermediary character. That character can be shown to be intimidated; the reader is not. The awkward journeys by which the cub pilot learns is different than the designed journey by which the reader learns.

By the end no one could doubt the depth and complexity of what a pilot must master. But there is no crash into a submerged tangle of syntactical snags or an exploding boiler of over-pressured prose. The text manages to replicate the way you learn to pilot the river without succumbing to an imitative fallacy by crushing the reader with particulars.

Twain does for the reader what his master Mr. Bixby did for him. "When I say I'll learn a man the river, I mean it. And you can depend on it, I'll learn him or kill him." In the end we don't of course learn the river; we learn how a Mississippi steamboat pilot goes about learning it. That's the point. The book is not a manual of piloting, but a remembrance of what piloting was like.[2]

5

Make 'Em Laugh, Make 'Em Laugh

In which we explore, with a smile, the possibilities with humor, word play, parody, and satire to expand the range of genres.

In *Singin' in the Rain*, Cosmo Brown (Donald O'Connor) attempts to rouse a despondent Don Lockwood (Gene Kelly) by appealing to humor. Make 'em laugh, make 'em laugh, he sings. You can dazzle the critics, charm with your erudition, quote Shakespeare, and starve, or you can slip on a banana peel and have the masses at your feet. There's a lot of uncomfortable truth in that observation. Humor works.

So much history, especially academic history, is written in the elevated intonations of High Seriousness. If the purpose is to declare the solemnity or epic stature of the work, the tone has its point. Yet a needlelike quip can puncture the most bloated balloon of Earnestness. A knock-knock joke can stay in the mind better than a syllogism. A pun can bring down an Emersonian epigram. (It says something that Plato's lectures did not survive but his popular entertainments, the dialogues, did.) If the purpose is to engage the reader quickly or to make a point, particularly by critiquing some prevailing thesis, consider humor, satire, parody, or just plain joking. An added benefit is that humor is almost always the shorter path.

Humor is plural, effective, memorable, accessible, and for writers of history generally a path not taken. Humor is hard to write. It is notoriously a matter of taste, which is to say, of audience. Some topics are in truth too awful to laugh away. Some prose has as its purpose to announce an Important Topic or a new voice of Serious Scholarship, though even here a sprinkling of comic wit can spice the text like a dash of chili pepper. The taste of the author, however, must agree with that of the audience.

There is not a lot of humorous nonfiction because most humor relies on tweaking the truth. Stuff is made up, stuff is left out, stuff is exaggerated up to and beyond the border of nonfiction, and of credence, and the result is not the Real Thing, but an obvious distortion, one that does not pretend it is anything else. Its point is to make us laugh, and for serious comics, to make us think by making us laugh. The text identifies itself as comedic: it's not fiction masquerading as nonfiction. Rather, humor seems to sit on a shelf that is its own.

Most nonfiction writers tend toward the earnest rather than the comedic. They may bury a chuckle in the text or include a sly smile in a metaphor, but humor seems alien. They are more likely to resort to irony rather than satire, and make the absurd dark rather than laughable. Still, humor is effective at arguing a point; satire and parody are genres that in particular lend themselves to literary nonfiction. And there is a place for comic relief, even in texts about writing. So let's grant a little space here for exaggeration, push beyond the bounds of nonfiction strictly defined, and enjoy a laugh.

Consider the following illustrations from the spice rack of humorous tropes.

History as Slapstick

W. C. Sellar and R. J. Yeatman, *1066 and All That: A Memorable History of England Comprising All the Parts You Can Remember, Including 103 Good Things, 5 Bad Kings and 2 Genuine Dates*

Canute, an Experimental King

This memorable monarch, having set out from Norway to collect some Danegeld, landed by mistake at Thanet, and thus became King.

Canute and the Waves

Canute began by being a Bad King on the advice of his Courtiers, who informed him (owing to a misunderstanding of the Rule Britannia) that the King of England was entitled to sit on the sea without getting wet. But finding that they were wrong he gave up this policy and decided to take his own advice in future—thus originating the memorable proverb, 'Paddle your own Canute'—and became a Good King and C. of E., and ceased to be memorable. After Canute there were no more aquatic kings till William IV (see later, Creation of Piers).

Canute had two sons, Halfacanute and Partacanute, and two other offspring, Rathacanute and Hardlicanute, who, however, he would never acknowledge, denying to the last that he was their Fathacanute.[1]

This is history as slapstick—a running gag of verbal pratfalls, conceptual cons, straight-man skits, malapropisms, and groaners. It's history as fractured by popular imagination and written for the Marx Brothers. At first blush it mocks the status of popular knowledge in which people mangle phrases and misappropriate names and generally confuse the order and causes of events. But a deeper reading might suggest that it equally mocks the Guild of Historians who have failed to provide meaningful handholds for the popular imagination and have thus ceded the field to the autodidacts and the Adderall junkies interested in the past. The style is effective at knocking the High Solemnity sect of the C. of H.

Still, a little of this—a very little (think jalapeños)—goes a long way. It's not a style that lends itself to close textual exegesis, so the less said about this farrago of bad puns, arbitrary capitalization, and misplaced allusions is probably to the good. Be warned.

Dave Barry, *Dave Barry Slept Here: A Sort of History of the United States*

Dave Barry's tour de farce of popular American history shows that the impulse to poke a stick in the eye of historians (if not History) didn't end with the Foundering Fathers. This book needs (okay, deserves) no introduction.

"The War to End All Wars"

President Wilson's theory at the time was that America would march over there and help France and Britain win the war, and then the winners would be extremely fair and decent and not take enormous sums of money or huge chunks of land from the losers, plus the entire system of world government would be reformed so that everybody would live in Peace and Freedom Forevermore. Needless to say, France and Britain thought this was the funniest theory they had ever heard, and they would beg Wilson to tell it again and again at dinner parties. "Hey Woody!" they'd shriek, tears of laughter falling into their cognac (CONE-yak). "Tell us the part where we don't take money or land!"

The Actual War Itself

The actual war itself was extremely depressing and in many cases fatal, so we're going to follow Standard History Textbook Procedure for talking about wars, under which we pretty much skip over the part where people get killed and instead make a big deal over what date the treaty was signed.

The Treaty of Versailles

The Treaty of Versailles (Pa-REE) was signed on a specific date—our guess would be October 8—and it incorporated Wilson's basic proposals, except that instead of *not* taking enormous sums of money and huge chunks of land from the losers, the winners at the last minute decided that it would be a better idea if they *did* take enormous sums of money and chunks of land from the losers. Other than that the war accomplished all of America's major objectives, and by 1919 Europe had been transformed, at a cost of only several million dead persons, from a group of nations that hated each other into a group of nations that *really* hated each other. Thus it came as no surprise when, in 1920, American voters overwhelmingly voted to elect a president named Warren G. Harding, who called for a return to 'normalcy,' which as far as we know is not even a real word.[2]

Popular wisdom holds that some things are so awful that the only sane response is to laugh. If Barry were inventing a past, his mockery would probably be unbearable if only for bad taste; but he is simply mangling the remembered past, which grants him some wiggle room.

The point here is to get a laugh. But who is the butt of the joke? Probably it's the absurd and eccentric way American history is recalled by the public, with whom Barry as authorial persona clearly identifies—no irony here—as it jumps from one catchphrase to another, as though Serious History were a string of commercial jingles. The laugh is not on history. It's on those who think they can mold public opinion by ideals, nailing down dates, or returning to a past that never existed (and is probably not a real word). At a minimum, the text must amuse. At best, it might inspire an occasional foray to a dictionary or genuine history to discover what all the confusion was about.

Philosophy as Stand-Up Comedy

Thomas Cathcart and Daniel Klein, *Plato and a Platypus Walk into a Bar . . . : Understanding Philosophy Through Jokes*

What the authors call "philogagging" makes a point about concepts and arguments. There is no reason why it can't be done with the stuff of history (except for taste, and maybe a delayed drumroll).

Here is a short gag on Leibniz's philosophy of rationalism.

From Leibniz's rationalist perspective, the world simply is what it is; the joke clarifies the obvious truth that optimism and pessimism are personal attitudes that have nothing do with Leibniz's neutral, rational description of the world.

The optimist says, "The glass is half full."
The pessimist says, "The glass is half empty."
The rationalist says, "The glass is twice as big as it needs to be."[3]

Or one that serves as a punch line to a clipped discourse on Platonic Virtue.

In his magnum opus, *The Republic*, Plato wrote, "The state is the soul writ large." So to discuss the virtues of the individual, he wrote a dialogue about the virtues of the ideal state. He called the rulers of this state philosopher kings, which may account for Plato's popularity with philosophers. The Philosopher Kings guide the state as Reason guides the human soul. The prime virtue—of both the PKs and Reason—is Wisdom, which Plato defined as understanding the Idea of the Good. However, one man's good is another man's goodies.

At a meeting of the college faculty, an angel suddenly appears and tells the head of the philosophy department, "I will grant you whichever of three blessings you choose: Wisdom, Beauty—or ten million dollars."

Immediately, the professor chooses Wisdom.

There is a flash of lightning, and the professor appears transformed, but he just sits there, staring down at the table. One of his colleagues whispers, "Say something."

The professor says, "I should have taken the money."[4]

Since joke writing is not part of professional training, most historians would be wise to quote their humor from the extant record, which shouldn't be hard since there's a lot out there. Not for nothing did Honoré Balzac title his serial novels *The Human Comedy*. It's one thing to record history's humor, and another to make it a joke. To keep it in bounds of professional propriety (if not scholarship), there should probably be some socially redeeming value to the witticism. Writers of historical fiction are quick to concede that the story comes first; the same is true of humor.

Enough said. Time now to shut down the open mic.

History as Humorous Story

Richard Feynman, *"Surely You're Joking, Mr. Feynman!"*

The least forced (and least painful) route to humor may simply be to tell a funny story. If it's short and has a punch line, it's a joke, and its point is to elicit a laugh. If it's longer and has a looser narrative structure, it's a humorous narrative, and its purpose may be to use a comic voice or perspective to present a theme or argue a thesis. The laughs may be silent or just mental chuckles.

Richard Feynman's memoir is based on anecdotes that he related and friends collected over the years. They read like yarns or tall tales. The voice is oral, the language conversational. Obviously, the transcripts have been edited since actual spoken language is almost impossible to read. Each story has a point, illustrates a feature of Feynman's worldview, and the pointillist composite does indeed, as the book's subtitle suggests, record the adventures of a "curious character." Feynman, a Nobel laureate in physics, is undoubtedly strange, but more significantly he is a character who is driven by curiosity.

Here—located centrally in the text—is his account of life at Los Alamos during the research that led to the atomic bomb. Out of necessity, pluckiness, and an irrepressible need to know, Feynman describes how he learned to pick safes.

I often went to Oak Ridge to check up on the safety of the uranium plant. Everything was always in a hurry because it was wartime, and one time I had to go there on a weekend. It was Sunday, and we were in this fella's office—a general, a head or a vice president of some company, a couple of other big muck-a-mucks, and me. We were gathered together to discuss a report that was in the fella's safe—a secret safe—when suddenly he realized that he didn't know the combination. His secretary was the only one who knew it, so he called her phone and it turned out she had gone on a picnic up in the hills.

While all this was going on, I asked, "Do you mind if I fiddle with the safe?"

"Ha, ha, ha—not at all!" So I went over to the safe and started to fool around.

They began to discuss how they could get a car to try to find the secretary, and the guy was getting more and more embarrassed because he had all these people waiting and he was such a jackass he didn't know how to open his own safe. Everybody was all tense and getting mad at him, when CLICK!—the safe opened.

In ten minutes I had opened the safe that contained all the secret documents about the plant. They were astonished. The safes were apparently not very safe. It was a terrible shock: All this "eyes only" stuff, top secret, locked in this wonderful secret safe, and this guy opens it in ten minutes![5]

Feynman then explains that he could perform the stunt only because he had spent several years poking, testing, practicing, and working out protocols, and that this safe happened to be one susceptible to what he had learned. The joke then turns on him. When he explains the trick, the officials decide that he is the problem, not defective safes and procedures. So ends his anecdote within a story.

In the end, in what becomes the whole story's climax, he contrives to meet an (unnamed) locksmith, whom he (Feynman) recognizes as the master safecracker of the community and who it turns out is just as eager to meet Feynman for the same reason. As they exchange experiences, they realize that they both rely on the same techniques and strategies. There is no magic or sleight of hand to the performance: safecracking relies on tested experience, study, logic, practice, and perseverance, which sounds a lot like how, in Feynman's mind, you do science. Learning to crack safes becomes an extended metaphor for cracking the locks and codes of nature. What makes the image vivid is that it comes wrapped in a story and narrated with a comical sense.

All in all, not a bad way to think about doing history as well.

Parody: The Sincerest Form of Insincere Praise

Typically the work of literary critics, and sensitive to stylistic quirks, parody works best when the author being parodied has a style so distinctive or idiosyncratic that it is easily recognized and copied even by amateurs. There are, for example, contests for faux Faulkner and bad Hemingway. But academic prose is also often distinctive and idiosyncratic (and as self-conscious about itself as "A Clean Well-Lighted Place" or *As I Lay Dying*); and it can be used to satirize both by taking serious what isn't and by mocking those who do take it too seriously, and bend their labored prose to show their seriousness.

Several illustrations follow. The first makes fun of bureaucracy and those who analyze it. The second deflates architectural ambition. The third demystifies the solemn way the professoriate discusses the central rite of academic passage, tenure. The fourth dumps two trendy passions, the locavore and the linguavore, into a common cauldron for skewering (excuse me, stewing). The desire for fresh food locally produced collides with the preference for Strunk-and-White-tinged linguistic purity. The last shows that even intellectual superstars can indulge in a little playful slumming.

C. Northcote Parkinson, "Parkinson's Law, or the Rising Pyramid"

Let Parkinson describe his purpose.

To the very young, to schoolteachers, as also to those who compile textbooks about constitutional history, politics, and current affairs, the world is a more or less rational place.... To those, on the other hand, with any experience of affairs, these assumptions are merely ludicrous. Solemn conclaves of the wise and good are mere figments of the teacher's mind. It is salutary, therefore, if an occasional warning is uttered on this subject. Heaven forbid that students should cease to read books on the science of public or business administration—provided only that these works are classified as fiction. Placed between the novels of Rider Haggard and H. G. Wells, intermingled with volumes about ape men and space ships, these textbook could harm no one.[6]

So here is his alternative, in practice:

What we have to note is that the 2000 officials of 1914 had become the 3569 of 1928; and that this growth was unrelated to any possible increase in their work. The Navy during that period had diminished, in point of fact, by a third in men and two-thirds in ships. Nor, from 1922 onward, was its strength even expected to increase; for its total of ships (unlike its total of officials) was limited by the Washington Naval Agreement of that year. Here we have then a 78 per cent increase over a period of fourteen years; an average of 5.6 per cent increase a year on the earlier total....

Can this rise in the total number of civil servants be accounted for except on the assumption that such a total must always rise by a law governing its growth?[7]

Parkinson is describing an astonishing, not to say outrageous, situation in which the size of the British Admiralty's staff increases without regard to the size of the operational fleet. The humor comes by presenting his observation in the deadpan, deadbeat prose of a scholar of public administration, which is to say, a social scientist.

The humor thus works two ways. Because the reader quickly sees the text as a spoof, Parkinson does not have to meet the standards of scholarly method, only to mimic it. Including a bogus formula completes the illusion since quantification is the highest goal of research; he can inject absurd comments—stuff he could never get away with in a straight op-ed piece. At the same time, his tone of querulous puzzlement and his massing of empirical details over what is an absurd situation mocks the whole apparatus of public administration as a discipline. Parkinson's Law makes a legitimate point—the tendency of bureaucracy, any bureaucracy, to grow as if from some internal compulsion. But if Parkinson had stated that fact baldly, he could sound like a grumpy ranter or a bean-counting scold. The kind of language he uses could just as easily numb into incoherence. Instead, a satirical voice and a parodic style make an argument not easily forgotten.

C. Northcote Parkinson, "Plans and Plants, or the Administration Block"[8]

In "Plans and Plants" he muses on the reverse phenomenon: the inevitable decay of institutions, symbolized by the creation of ideal settings for them to operate in. The more completely realized the edifice, the more nearly the organization has peaked, or more likely passed its prime. The examples pile up, all historical. It's hard to say why the result is funny—he's describing major features of human society, after all, and they are bumbling about in profound self-ignorance as their wish to express their ideal clashes with their actual ability to perform. But after reading his piece, no one can look at St. Peter's Square or the U.N. building in the same way as before.

> It is now known that a perfection of planned layout is achieved only by institutions on the point of collapse. This apparently paradoxical conclusion is based upon a wealth of archaeological and historical research, with the more esoteric details of which we need not concern ourselves. In general principle, however, the method pursued has been to select and date the buildings which appear to have been perfectly designed

for their purpose. A study and comparison of these has tended to prove that perfection of planning is a symptom of decay. During a period of exciting discovery or progress there is no time to plan the perfect head-quarters. The time for that comes later, when all the important work has been done. Perfection, we know, is finality; and finality is death.

Next he gives the principle a particular as illustration:

Thus, to the casual tourist, awestruck in front of St. Peter's, Rome, the Basilica and the Vatican must seem the ideal setting for the Papal Mon-archy at the very height of its prestige and power. Here, he reflects, must Innocent III have thundered his anathema. Here must Gregory VII have laid down the law. But a glance at the guidebook will convince the traveler that the really powerful Popes reigned long before the present dome was raised, and reigned not infrequently somewhere else. More than that, the later Popes lost half their authority while the work was still in progress. Julius II, whose decision it was to build, and Leo X, who approved Raphael's design, were dead long before the buildings assumed their present shape. Bramante's palace was still building until 1565, the great church not consecrated until 1626, nor the piazza colon-nades finished until 1667. The great days of the Papacy were over before the perfect setting was even planned. They were almost forgotten by the date of its completion.[9]

Andy Bryan, "Back from Yet Another Globetrotting Adventure, Indiana Jones Checks His Mail and Discovers That His Bid for Tenure Has Been Denied"

Here the parody is academic prose in its bureaucratic avatar. The flat cadences roll somnolently on, like a droning lecture, the style wildly at odds with its substantive content, as the readers will immediately under-stand. Both prose and profession are mocked.

January 22, 1939

Assistant Professor Henry "Indiana" Jones Jr.
Department of Anthropology
Chapman Hall 227B
Marshall College

Dr. Jones:

As chairman of the Committee on Promotion and Tenure, I regret to inform you that your recent application for tenure has been denied by a vote of 6 to 1. Following past policies and procedures, proceedings from the committee's deliberations that were pertinent to our decision have been summarized below according to the assessment criteria.

Demonstrates suitable experience and expertise in chosen field:

The committee concurred that Dr. Jones does seem to possess a nearly superhuman breadth of linguistic knowledge and an uncanny familiarity with the history and material culture of the occult. However, his understanding and practice of archaeology gave the committee the greatest cause for alarm. Criticisms of Dr. Jones ranged from "possessing a perceptible methodological deficiency" to "practicing archaeology with a complete lack of, disregard for, and colossal ignorance of current methodology, theory, and ethics" to "unabashed graverobbing." Given such appraisals, perhaps it isn't surprising to learn that several Central and South American countries recently assembled to enact legislation aimed at permanently prohibiting his entry.

Moreover, no one on the committee can identify who or what instilled Dr. Jones with the belief that an archaeologist's tool kit should consist solely of a bullwhip and a revolver.

So it goes through the obligatory roll call of professional expectations: a nationally recognized program of scholarship, the high-caliber publications, diligence and success in teaching, service to department, college, and profession.

Meets professional standards of conduct in research and professional activities of the discipline:
The committee was particularly generous (and vociferous) in offering their opinions regarding this criterion. Permit me to list just a few of the more troubling accounts I was privy to during the committee's meeting. Far more times than I would care to mention, the name "Indiana Jones" (the adopted title Dr. Jones insists on being called) has appeared in governmental reports linking him to the Nazi Party, black-market antiquities dealers, underground cults, human sacrifice, Indian child slave labor, and the Chinese mafia. There are a plethora of international criminal charges against Dr. Jones, which include but are not limited to: bringing unregistered weapons into and out of the country; property damage; desecration of national and historical landmarks; impersonating officials; arson; grand theft (automobiles, motorcycles, aircraft, and watercraft in just a one week span last year); excavating without a permit; countless antiquities violations; public endangerment; voluntary and involuntary manslaughter; and, allegedly, murder.

The committee's conclusion is inevitable:

To summarize, the committee fails to recognize any indication that Dr. Jones is even remotely proficient when it comes to archaeological scholarship and practice. His aptitude as an instructor is questionable at best, his conduct while abroad is positively deplorable, and his behavior on campus is minimally better. Marshall College has a reputation to uphold. I need not say more.

My apologies,

Prof. G. L. Stevens
Chairman[10]

Style and story—what is being told must align with the how of
its telling. So goes the most elementary of guidelines for good prose.
But in the passage above, a wild disparity arises between the formal,
cautious wording of a letter from a tenure review committee and the
subject they are charged to discuss, someone far beyond the pale of
academic norms. Style and subject don't match, and that is how the
parody derives its power. Again, the passage goes two ways. It exposes
the absurdity of Jones as a professor—he does nothing appropriate
to his status and standing. But it also ridicules a klatch of colleagues
who cannot see any value in his exploits and cannot wrestle them into
language suitable to a faculty position. The misfit may make for a bad
hire but it's good humor.

Michael Erard, "A Pledge to My Readers"

> I've always written high-quality sentences, prepared with the finest
> grammatical ingredients. In the coming year, I'm raising the bar even
> higher: I'll be offering only artisanal words, locally grown, hand-picked,
> minimally processed, organically prepared, and sustainably packaged.
>
> Readers no longer know where the words they read and hear come
> from, how they're produced, or who produces them, but I'm going to
> help change that, because good artisanal writing begins with healthy
> local materials. For nouns, I'm going to a nearby family-owned farm,
> where Anglo-Saxon and Latinate varieties are raised free-range, grass-
> fed, and entirely hormone-free. The farmers will regularly replenish my
> stocks with deliveries by bicycle, ensuring that these words ripen on the
> page, not in a cargo hold in the middle of the Pacific.

Getting fresh, organic verbs used to pose a challenge, because of the unusual way they propagate. Yet once I began searching out indigenous varieties of words, I was surprised to find all sorts that aren't known outside the local area. There's a small, family-run verb operation that conjugates them in small batches, the old-fashioned way. I also stumbled across a number of hard-to-find heirloom verbs that haven't been seen in urban markets for 100 years, because their flesh bruises too easily, and because they don't fit the cosmetic ideal. Let's face it: An English verb grown in Chile may look perfectly connoted, but its pulpy taste can't compete with the pungent verve of a local specimen, and who cares if it won't win beauty contests....

A century ago, writers in major cities like Boston and New York had all the function words they needed grown less than 100 miles away, but now 95% of them are imported. Did you know that the typical auxiliary verb has to travel more than 1,500 miles to reach the writer who uses it? As the world has become more interconnected, it's become frighteningly easy to ship words from nearly anywhere, and they often cost more to read than to deliver. The rise of cheap, factory-produced, highly processed words has led to a rise in unhealthy reading, and has also damaged local systems of word production that once were our nation's pride....

Also, I recycle.[11]

"Also, I recycle"—a nice coda that helps place the putative author into the moral landscape, or the fads that can serve as proxies for a moral sense, while further ridiculing his misplaced earnestness.

So who or what is being mocked? Everything, it seems—literary taste, foodies, political correctness, the trendiness of declarations regarding personal ethics. What makes the skewering possible is the deadpan style of earnestness in which the writer seemingly fails to appreciate the absurdity of his appeal. The organizing metaphor is not simply extended but misplaced. The entire piece is a malapropism. It's also short—a tapas bar, not a banquet—which is fortunate because a longer piece would be indigestible.

Umberto Eco, "How to Travel on American Trains" and "How to Write an Introduction"

Yes, even elite writers, esteemed professors of semiotics, can usefully indulge in satire and slum their hours away in writing parody. For years Umberto Eco wrote a short column, the *Diario minimo*, for newspapers. The best pieces he gathered from time to time into anthologies. He lists them under his nonfiction works.

In a preface he observes, "For such is the fate of parody: it must never fear exaggerating. If it strikes home, it will only prefigure something that others will then do without a smile—and without a blush—in steadfast, virile seriousness." Below are two samples in which, true to his word, Eco treads fearlessly into exaggeration.[12]

American trains are the image of what the world might be like after an atomic war. It isn't that the trains don't leave, it's that of they don't arrive, having broken down en route, causing people to wait during a six-hour delay in enormous stations, icy and empty, without a snack bar, inhabited by suspicious characters, and riddled with underground passages that recall the scenes in the New York subways in *Return to the Planet of the Apes*. The line between New York and Washington, patronized by newspaper reporters and senators, in first class offers at least business-class comfort, with a tray of hot food worthy of a university dining hall. But other lines have filthy coaches, with eviscerated leatherette cushions, and the snack bar offers food that makes you nostalgic (you'll say I'm exaggerating) for the recycled saw dust you are forced to eat on the Milan-Rome express....

The train, in America, is not a choice. It is a punishment for, having neglected to read Weber on the Protestant ethic and the spirit of capitalism, making the mistake of remaining poor.[13]

And not to be neglected in a guide to writing, consider Eco's take on writing introductions for books published "by a university press or its equivalent." The critical component is the acknowledgments: "for skill in making acknowledgments is the hallmark of the thoroughbred scholar." It can sometimes happen, he admits, "that a scholar, his task completed, discovers he has no one to thank. Never mind. He will invent some debts. Research without indebtedness is suspect, and somebody must always, somehow, be thanked." Eco then proceeds to thank everyone imaginable who in some fashion, however tenuous the filament, contributed to his introduction to introductions.[14]

It's a long and tedious list. All the educational institutions that support him, his secretary, his editors, his wife ("who, always ready with the reassurance that all is vanity, was—and is—able to tolerate the moods and demands of a scholar constantly obsessed by the major problems of existence"), his children, the board of directors of *L'Espresso*, Olivetti, MicroPro, Wordstar 2000 (Eco may be the only human in history to thank that benighted software), his Okidata Microline 182 printer, and various English-language editors "who have sustained me with heartwarming and pressing daily telephone calls, informing me that the presses were rolling and, that at all costs, I had to provide the final footnotes." He ends with the ritual self-abnegation that any errors are his alone.[15]

Yes, but so are the surprises, and the successes.

Satire

Whether or not history is absurd in the round, the past certainly abounds with absurdities. They can be used to make a point, or a point can be made by pushing ideas, people, and events to the threshold of inanity, and when the absurdities don't exist, they can be created by shaping how the past is presented. That exaggeration is what makes satire work, even if, technically, it pushes the text outside the domain of nonfiction.

Washington Irving, *Knickerbocker's History of New York*

The elevated style can be the equivalent of some rube walking around with a sign on his backside that reads *Kick me*. Washington Irving mocks the pretense in his *Knickerbocker's History of New York*, in which Peter Stuyvesant becomes a laughable echo of Plutarch's Great Men. But it is the nominal historian, Dietrich Knickerbocker, the putative author of it all, who becomes the object of the longest running joke by trying to make epic what is by most standards banal.

He likens himself to the "great Father of History," Herodotus, and he proclaims, without the slightest self-consciousness, "Thrice happy, therefore, is this our renowned city, in having incidents worthy of swelling the theme of history; and doubly thrice happy is it in having such an historian as myself to relate them. For after all, gentle reader, cities of themselves, and, in fact, empires of themselves, are nothing without an historian." It is the "patient narrator who records their prosperity as they rise—who blazons forth the splendor of their noontide meridian—who props their feeble memorials as they totter to decay—who gathers together their scattered fragments as they rot—and who piously, at length, collects their ashes into the mausoleum of his work, and rears a triumphant monument to transmit their renown to all succeeding ages." So it is he imagines his history of New York marching on like "Gibbon's Rome, or Hume and Smollett's England!" like a "gallant commander, to honor and immortality." Appropriately, Knickerbocker expires, after arranging his affairs, in the arms of his old friend, the librarian.[16]

The history itself has its eye on the epic, full of classical allusions and inflated rhetoric, a muted Homer. Here he describes the Achilles-like Peter Stuyvesant in the heat of battle.

> But what, O Muse! was the rage of Peter Stuyvesant, when from afar he saw his army giving way! In the transports of his wrath he sent forth a roar, enough to shake the very hills. The men of the Manhattoes plucked

up new courage at the sound; or rather, they rallied at the voice of their leader, of whom they stood more in awe than of all the Swedes in Christendom. Without waiting for their aid, the daring Peter dashed, sword in hand, into the thickest of the foe. Then might be seen achievements worthy of the days of the giants. Wherever he went, the enemy shrank before him; the Swedes fled to right and left, or were driven, like dogs, into their own ditch; but, as he pushed forward singly with headlong courage, the foe closed behind and hung upon his rear. One aimed a blow full at his heart; but the protecting power which watches over the great and the good turned aside the hostile blade, and directed it to a side pocket, where reposed an enormous iron tobacco-box, endowed, like the shield of Achilles, with supernatural powers, doubtless from bearing the portrait of the blessed St. Nicholas. Peter Stuyvesant turned like an angry bear upon the foe, and seizing him as he fled, by an immeasurable queue, "Ah, whoreson caterpillar," roared he, "here's what shall make worms' meat of thee!" So saying, he whirled his sword, and dealt a blow that would have decapitated the varlet, but that the pitying steel struck short, and shaved the queue for ever from his crown. At this moment an arquebusier leveled his piece from a neighboring mound, with deadly aim; but the watchful Minerva, who had just stopped to tie up her garter, seeing the peril of her favorite hero, sent old Boreas with his bellows, who, as the match descended to the pan, gave a blast that blew the priming from the touch-hole.[17]

In the end it is Dietrich Knickerbocker who bears the brunt of the burlesque, for it is he who renders New Amsterdam into a new Troy, Stuyvesant's cast-of-dozens skirmish into a costume drama set piece, and a narrative taking its inspiration from Thucydides into something out of *Duck Soup*. In his mind, however, without proper attention Stuyvesant's story will melt into a haze of legendry like those "of Romulus and Remus, of Charlemagne, King Arthur, Rinaldo, and Godfrey of Boulogne." (Say again?) The more exalted the literary language, the more hysterically at odds it is with reality, and the more the *Knickerbocker's History* reads less like a scene out of Shakespeare than a skit lifted from *Saturday Night Live*.

At this point poor Dietrich Knickerbocker stands for all historians whose stories overshadow their sources, whose ambitions reach beyond the grasp of their judgment, and whose elevated diction floats over the rainbow. Dietrich Knickerbocker is the historian as Don Quixote. In such circumstances a gentle mockery may be the only balm.

P. J. O'Rourke, *All the Troubles in the World*

Genuine satire demands more than stand-up one-liners: it plays against expectations and conventions. In *Knickerbocker's History*, the straight man is not just popular history, in all its inventive foolishness, but the belief that Serious History can transcend the populist tendency to dumb down and mix up, or that people can handle historical understanding with more sophistication than they can the weeds in their backyard. Because he positions himself among the crowd, as one of the unwashed and unlettered, Dave Barry blunted the edge of his satire. He ended up siding with the reader against the solemnity of the professionals.

Still, his is a Horacian satire grounded in a world of bumblers and fools. Other satirists use a razor wit to go for the jugular. A contemporary master is P. J. O'Rourke, whose mockery, besides carrying *reductio ad absurdum* to new depths of *absurda*, strops against what are supposed to be serious affairs of state and society. The surface text may be O'Rourke's misadventures among the delusional (and hence dangerous), but the subtext is politics. Most of what happens or what he observes isn't funny: it becomes satirical by being pushed beyond logic and common sense. Unlike Barry he is not among the crowd, but on its margins, as befits a satyr, throwing rocks at the pretense. There is nothing balanced or fair about his treatment. The argument relies on exaggeration, which becomes tolerable only insofar as it is comic. If it's

funny, it's satire. If it's not funny, it's just a rant, and it is unlikely to move
the needle of public opinion any more than traditional hand-wringing.
Here O'Rourke turns his gimlet eye on rainforests and the environ-
mentalism that has made them sacrosanct.

I have accumulated a three-foot stack of books and articles about the
rain forest. (Just think of the dead trees. And, by the way, do you send a
decorative arrangement of cement to a plant funeral?) From this reading material, I gather that, if the rain forest disappears, we'll have to get
our air in little bottles from the Evian company, and biodiversity will
vanish, and pretty soon we'll only have about one kind of animal, and
with my luck that will be the Lhasa apso. The indigenous people will all
become exdigenous and move to L.A....

This is the rainforest as meme. How about the rainforest as ecological
entity?

In my reading about the rain forest, however, I have found very little
description of what it is like to actually *be* in a rain forest. There's a good
reason for this, the same reason that little girls' baby dolls don't actually
smell like babies. Not that the rain forest smells. You'd think something
so wet, hot and biological would stink like boiled Times Square, but
it doesn't. Jungle has a nice fresh sent, the reason being that there's so
much life in the jungle that anything which dies or is excreted or even
gets drowsy is immediately a picnic for something else....
  The intense, even NBA-like competition among living things in the
rain forest means that almost every plant and animal has some kind
of stinger, barb, thorn, prickle, spur, spine, poison, or angry advocacy
group back in the United States boycotting your place of business.
There's a fierce competition for the nutrients in the ground, which is
why rain-forest soil is notoriously poor and easily damaged by horti-
culture. The tremendous hardwood trees of the jungle, rising 120 feet
with prodigious rocket-ship tail-fin buttresses and trunks as big around

as tract houses, are rooted in earth where you couldn't grow petunias. It's hard to imagine something so enormous and complex based upon virtually nothing. Unless you've had experience with large American corporations.[18]

Clearly, O'Rourke isn't mocking rainforest: it just is. He's mocking the attitudes of those who have created an idealist notion of it, a vision that also conveys a particular political sensibility for causes he dislikes. Not being an equal opportunity mocker, anyone to the left of Libertarianism is apt to be skewered somewhere in his trek through the jungle.

David Brooks, "The Real Romney"

Best known as an editorial columnist, and for an aura of high earnestness, David Brooks here plays against type in his profile of presidential candidate Mitt Romney.

> Mitt Romney was born on March 12, 1947, in Ohio, Florida, Michigan, Virginia and several other swing states. He emerged, hair first, believing in America, and especially its national parks. He was given the name Mitt, after the Roman god of mutual funds, and launched into the world with the lofty expectation that he would someday become the Arrow shirt man.
>
> Romney was a precocious and gifted child. He uttered his first words ("I like to fire people") at age 14 months, made his first gaffe at 15 months and purchased his first nursery school at 24 months. The school, highly leveraged, went under, but Romney made 24 million Jujubes on the deal.[19]

And a couple of other quips:

> The teenage years were more turbulent. He was sent to a private school, where he was saddened to find there are people in America who

summer where they winter. He developed a lifelong concern for the second homeless, and organized bake sales with proceeds going to the moderately rich.

Some have said Romney's lifestyle is overly privileged, pointing to the fact that he has an elevator for his cars in the garage of his San Diego home. This is not entirely fair. Romney owns many homes without garage elevators and the cars have to take the stairs.

This is a standard profile based on telling details. Romney is known for his chiseled features (and handsome hair), his privileged upbringing, his MBA rise to riches, and his family, which by being ultratraditional, is actually nontraditional in today's America. Brooks takes each of these traits and distorts them by pushing them to an (il-)logical end. Every feature of Romney's political biography that his campaign has promoted as an asset becomes a liability. For all his talents and virtues, Mitt Romney is simply not a man of the people, as Brooks's concluding line makes clear. "If elected, he promises to bring all Americans together and make them feel inferior."

Tom Wolfe, *The Kingdom of Speech*

Now watch another gifted satirist turn his weaponized rhetoric—a Wolfean howl, as it were—against the cherished story of how Charles Darwin discovered natural evolution.

Satire requires contrast, and here the contrasts are two. One is between ideas and facts, between those who think and those who fuse thinking with doing. Wolfe sneers at the closet thinkers and cheers on those who are up to their necks in a messy world for which there are barely words, much less theories about how those words happened. (Clearly, Wolfe as writer identifies with those tramping the world out there rather than those workshopping prose in air-conditioned seminar rooms.) The other contrast is between the presumed power of science, especially its claim to explain what makes us human, and its inability to account for language, which Wolfe claims is what has made humans so dominant on Earth.

Charles Darwin and evolution. It's a topic of High Seriousness, a pivotal point in intellectual history, the moment biology moved beyond butterfly catching and became a real science and the moment organized religion began to sink into a comedic sideshow. The Saga of Darwin is oft retold, almost an obligatory prelude, like Old Testament Prophets retelling the story of Exodus to establish their credentials before declaiming their new insight or outrage. In this case, while the Saga of Darwin has its serial climaxes, the most celebrated may be the arrival of a personal letter to Darwin written by Alfred Wallace, then down with malaria in the Malay Archipelago, in which he outlines the theory of evolution by natural selection. Darwin has had his own sketch of the same idea, based on the same insights, kept in a locked drawer for twenty-one years. He stands to lose priority. In the Saga he rises to the occasion honorably and arranges for Wallace to share priority by having both their papers read to the same meeting of the Linnaean Society. By the time Wallace, unaware of what has transpired, returns to Britain, Darwin has written *On the Origin of Species*, and we have Darwinism, not Wallacism.

It's a pivotal moment in Wolfe's retelling, too, but rather than address it with scholarly solemnity, arguing thesis by thesis, fact by counterfact, he lampoons the topic with two standard satirical devices. One is to attack the character of the founder, in this case Darwin. The other is to ridicule the arguments and evidence. "Attack" takes the form of a retelling, with the frame askew so that the accepted facts lose their inherited stability and look awkward, even foolish. Assumptions rooted in a deep duff of Darwinian folklore become unsettled. Wolfe reduces a Solemn Theory of Everything to just words—myths, metaphors, Just So Stories, a "real tour de force of literary imagination," "sincere, but sheer, literature." He reduces a cosmogeny of Modernity to speech, which is his theme, and his home turf. He's not competing with Darwinism as science. He's competing with it as literature.

Wolfe narrates that moment by placing it within a society of Victorian Gentlemen, a class system to which Darwin is a full member and Wallace a rude "flycatcher."

Oh, Charlie, Charlie, Charlie ... said Lyell, shaking his head, who was it who warned you two years ago about this fellow Wallace? Who was it who told you you'd better get busy and publish this pet theory of yours? ... So why should I even bother, this late in the game?

But we *are* Gentlemen and old pals, after all ... and I think I know of a way to get you out of this predicament. It so happens there is a meeting of the Linnean Society postponed from last month in deference to the death of one of our beloved former Linnean presidents, coming up *thirteen days from now*, July 1. Unfortunately, we don't have any way to notify Wallace in time, do we. But that's not *our* fault. *We* didn't schedule the meeting. That's just the way it goes sometimes. We'll bring our good friend Sir Joseph Dalton Hooker, the botanist, in on this. All three of us are on the society's council. We can make the whole thing seem like the most routine scholarly meeting in the world ... the usual learned papers learned papers learned papers, the usual *drone drone drone humm drumm humm* ... The main thing, Charlie, is to establish your priority. We'll present your work *and* Wallace's. Now, that's fair, isn't it? Even-steven and all that? Well, to be perfectly frank, there *is* one slight hitch. You've never published a line of your work on Evolution. Not one line. As far as the scientific world at large is aware, you have never *done* any. You don't even have a paper to present at the meeting ... *hmmm* ... Ahh! I know! We can help you create an abstract overnight! An *abstract*. Get it?[20]

Darwin is "aghast." "I should be *extremely* glad *now* to publish a sketch of my general views in about a dozen pages or so," he wrote Lyell. "But I cannot persuade myself that I can do so honorably. . . . I would far rather burn my whole book than that he or any man should think that I had behaved in a paltry spirit."

Or that "was my first impression," he says to Lyell, suddenly switching gears, "& I should have certainly acted on it, had it not been for your letter." But your *letter* . . . *your* letter has shown the way. *Even Stephen,* you have ruled. *Even Stephen!* And who am I to presume to overrule Sir Charles Lyell? You are the dean of British naturalists, my old friend. There is no greater or wiser man in this entire field. Everyone, including Wallace, will be better off in the end if we leave all this in your accomplished hands.[21]

The "one remaining catch," Wolfe wryly notes, is that "Lyell and Hooker expected Darwin to write his own abstract."

He couldn't do that—he *mustn't* do that. He begged off with some pathetic excuse. He didn't have the courage to tell them that his own conscience must be kept clear. His *own conscience* had to believe he had nothing to do with this project. It wasn't *his* idea. It was entirely theirs, Lyell's and Hooker's. I, Charles Darwin, *had nothing to do with it!* Above all, let no man be able to say I wrote an abstract for myself after reading Wallace's paper. There mustn't be a hint of any such paltriness before an august body like the Linnean.

So it fell upon Lyell's and Hooker's shoulders, the task of concocting for Charlie an abstract out of what they could lay their hands on quickly. . . .[22]

Wolfe concludes by turning the project inside out.

To put the matter in perspective, one has only to imagine what would have happened had the roles been reversed. Suppose Darwin is the one who has just written a formal twenty-page scientific treatise for publication . . . and somehow Wallace gets his hands on it ahead of time . . . and announces that he made this same astounding epochal discovery twenty-one years ago but just never got around to writing it up and claiming priority . . . a horse laugh? He wouldn't have rated anything that hearty. Maybe a single halfway-curled upper lip, if anybody deigned to notice at all.[23]

In Wolfe's retelling, the elevated language of a Great Moment in History becomes colloquial chatter, the august Sir Charles becomes "Charlie," and the grand bargain over copublication becomes a backroom conspiracy. Darwin the Undaunted, boldly throwing down the gauntlet before a benighted public, is reduced to a simpering pleader, horrified that his dalliance might lose him priority and petrified that his caste might think him "paltry" and so lets his pals do the work for him and then take the heat while he nurtures his hypochondria, with his conscience not completely at ease but his hunger for fame without regrets.

Wolfe wants to place human speech, language, at the core of what separates humans from other animals. He doesn't object to evolution: he celebrates its discovery, but unhinges it from Darwinism by shifting attention to Wallace. What he opposes is the *ism* that has attached to it, that makes it a Theory of Everything, because he is convinced that it cannot explain speech. Evolution as cosmogeny is simply myth. A universal language organ somewhere, somehow in the brain, as postulated by Noam Chomsky, is metaphor. It's all literature.

Is it fair? Of course not. That's what makes it satire. Wolfe's intellectual takedown of Darwin (and later, Chomsky) is sure to infuriate those partisans devoted to evolution as cosmogeny and those committed to the scientific method as the only means of positive knowledge. Wolfe doesn't debate the case on their terms. He debates it on his. And in the Kingdom of Speech, he who can write, who understands how to match genre with theme, who knows how language can carry meaning beyond the definitions of separate words by the artistry with which they are used, who has mastered speech among people as humans have among creation, he wins. In truth, the contest isn't all that close.

6

Deep Details, Thick Descriptions

In which we explore how to write on technical topics without getting lost in thickets of description.

Technical topics might range from spinning skeins of wool to explicating competing templates of time. What makes them technical is not just the subject itself but the kind of knowledge a writer can assume the reader brings to the text. Some topics lend themselves better to visuals than to words—nautical knots, for example, or running a pump. But many notions, and much of historical evidence, come out of texts, and lots of topics will deal with ideas. The useful question for writers is how to convert abstractions into memorable prose.

The possible techniques are many. Some will involve narrative, but narrative is not the only or sometimes best way to describe thickly or with deep details. When a lot of information has to be presented compactly, when a topic is best explained by contrast, or when there are points of logic and argument to make, another strategy may work best. In a celebrated essay, "A Place for Stories," William Cronon made a powerful case for the role of storytelling, but rather than illustrate his point by organizing his theme as a story, he gives it the form of an argument.

Each of the following examples has a different purpose and audience. But each has adopted a design and style suitable to that intent and the intended readership.

Detail Through Personification

G. W. Whitrow, *The Natural Philosophies of Time*

What is time? It's intuitively obvious—everyone has a sense of time. Yet it is also maddeningly difficult to define in a scientific and philosophical sense. G. W. Whitrow's magisterial inquiry is a study in how Western civilization has conceptualized time as a natural phenomenon—not exactly a book headed for Hollywood and action figures with Happy Meals. This is a serious book for a select audience.

The design is a very common one in scholarship: it's the basic formula for most dissertations. It introduces a thesis; it masses evidence and arguments as it examines one concept after another; it concludes with the author's judgment about how to resolve the thesis. The concepts could as easily be eras, or profiles of characters, or examinations of building architecture. The point of view is that of an omniscient observer, mastering material that spans a couple thousand years and restating it in a common idiom. It spans topics from Zeno's paradoxes to circadian rhythms to relativity. The order of chapters is not arbitrary, but neither is it driven by chronology; the story of time is here not itself a story. The chapters follow like logs in a corduroy bridge. It's a scholarly model, though one done well. The book even includes some equations (an appendix includes a derivation of the Lorentz formulae). This is not a text for the casual reader.

Yet it is completely accessible to a committed one. The trick is to get the reader to commit. Whitrow does this by introducing the topic through personification. A slogging complexity is reduced to two competing understandings of nature, personified by Archimedes and Aristotle, one that ignores time and one that makes time an informing principle. The personification is subtle: the text is not about people, who have certain ideas, but ideas, which are best expressed by certain people. The abstruse becomes concrete, the complex memorable; and a reader not already versed in the disciplinary nuances can ease into a potentially formidable subject.

The history of natural philosophy is characterized by the interplay of two opposing points of view which may be conveniently associated with the names of Archimedes and of Aristotle, those intellectual giants of antiquity whose writing were of decisive important for the late medieval and Renaissance founders of modern science. Archimedes is the prototype of those whose philosophy of physics presupposes the "elimination" of time, i.e., of those who believe that temporal flux is not an intrinsic feature of the ultimate basis of things. Aristotle, on the other hand, is the forerunner of those who regard time as fundamental, since he insisted that there are real "comings-into-being" and that the world has a basic temporal structure.[1]

There follows a paragraph that explains more specifically what each man did and what it meant to subsequent generations. "Archimedes was the founder of the science of hydrostatics and the author of the first important treatise of statics. What Euclid did for the art of the stonemason, Archimedes did for the practical and intuitive knowledge of generations of technicians who had operated simple machines like the balance and the lever. He laid bare the theoretical basis of this knowledge and, following the example of Euclid, presented it as a logically coherent system." His treatise *On the Equilibrium of Planes* remains an "ideal" of a "scientific discipline based on rigorous argument from apparently incontrovertible premises," but the concept of time played no part in it.

"Aristotle's treatment of physical problems was very different." It was based on movement, on growth, in which "everything that is in motion must be moved by something," a formulation "which had to be rejected before an effective science of dynamics" could be formulated. "Nevertheless, with all its faults," Aristotle's physics was in one vital respect superior to that of Archimedes.

The certainty and lucidity of Archimedes' principles are largely due to the fact that they are gathered, so to speak, from the surface of phenomena and not dug out from the depths. His logically perfect treatise on statics was, in fact, less profound and less rich in promise of fruitful developments than the immature and disorderly work of Aristotle. The reason for this is clear: Archimedes avoided the problem of motion; Aristotle faced them. In the natural philosophy of Archimedes laws of nature are laws of equilibrium and temporal concepts play no part, whereas for Aristotle nature was "a principle of motion and change" and could not be understood without an analysis of time.[2]

The Natural Philosophy of Time is a long and potentially dismal survey of the various conceptual approaches to time. It's easy to imagine an unthinking opening that baldly states that time is a difficult topic with a long history of conflicting conceptions, which then proceeds to lay out, perhaps with bullet points, the arguments used for and against the various imaginings. The outcome might well be useful to specialists as a reference work. It would interest no one else.

In fact, the text reads clearly and relatively briskly. Why? The intellectual tension of the two fundamental traditions, the Archimedean and the Aristotelean, creates something like a loose dialectic. Their contrasting perspectives make the question of time engaging in ways that a flat declaration of a thesis would not. Specialists will have to read out of scholarly obligation. Interested lay persons will read because the introduction lays down a kind of intellectual contest and they will want to see how it unfolds.

Detail Through Taxonomy

Woodbridge Riley, *American Thought from Puritanism to Pragmatism and Beyond*

Look now at a very different kind of opening for a book with a very different conception of events through time. History is an evolutionary unfolding of events with something like a direction to it, and as befits a progressive like Woodbridge Riley, that sequence is one of general improvement. Chapter follows chapter, but in an order that cannot be rearranged, what Riley in another book called "the march of the mind," as American thought follows an arc from Puritanism to Pragmatism. The text exudes a conviction and directness that suggests history had to move this way, and that it has to be written about in the way Riley does.

Riley's purpose is to demonstrate that America has "had philosophers, original thinkers who, though their influence may not have reached abroad, were makers of history at home." Studying them will sharpen understanding "of our national character," for these developments are "so closely allied to our history and our literature that they may be said to form a background for both." In particular, philosophy has influenced politics. Here resides the intellectual and moral energy behind the history: ideas matter because they affect politics, which is to say, the arrangement of power in the American polity.[3]

His opening—"Philosophy and Politics, from Absolutism to Democracy"—brazenly, if breezily, shows how this happens.

> The influence of philosophy upon politics in America is easily seen in the evolution of such a familiar phrase as life, liberty, and the pursuit of happiness. This declaration of independence was derived indirectly, by way of reaction, from a declaration of dependence. The belief of the Puritans was a belief in passivity, determinism, and pessimism. They considered that man was a mere worm, a dull instrument in the hands of Deity; that his acts were predestined, Deity foreordaining whatsoever comes to pass; that his life was a vain show, and nature a vale of tears. Over against these lugubrious doctrines of the Puritans we may put those of their successors. It was the deists who believed in activity, freedom, and optimism. They held that man was a real agent; that he was free to do what he chose; that his goal was perfection itself, and they even went so far as to say that whatever is, is right. These beliefs slowly spread among the people and were gradually translated into the plain

language of the day. Instead of passivity the deists believed in activity,—
that is, life; instead of determinism they believed in freedom,—that is,
liberty; instead of pessimism they believed in optimism,—that is, the
pursuit of happiness. In short, between the Boston Platform of 1680 and
the Declaration of Independence of 1776 a marked change had come
about. The deistic sun had arisen, dispelling the winter of Puritan dis-
content. Humanity was considered perfectible, and this world the best
of all possible worlds.[4]

A great deal of scholarly water has flowed under the bridge of these
themes since Riley wrote, and his pronouncements today seem closer to
historical caricature than to national character. Professional historians
would demand more nuance, more qualifications, perhaps more empa-
thy for the historical characters. But probably what would raise hackles
in academics is the conviction in his voice and the rigid structure of rhetoric. Possibly tone and trope need each other: the flow of his enthusiasms would spill across the page without careful levees to contain them.
The clear contrast illustrates what the author sees as a conflict among
competing ideas that has political consequences, one that speaks to his
own Progressive Era.

This is a book for serious readers who are not specialists. Riley isn't
arguing his case: he's presenting his conclusions to a wider audience,
and his appeal to classic literary devices is a way to distill and accent
what he wants to say. Consider another passage in which he sums up
some influences on pragmatism as a way to place William James in philosophical traditions.

We have gone through the forerunners of pragmatism, ancient, medieval, and modern, and have discovered that the pragmatists, although
contemners of the past, have had numerous predecessors. With the
sophistic doctrine their affinities are more than superficial, with the
nominalistic more than nominal. But with the modern the perspective
is closer and distinctions loom into differences. Although pragmatism

is so largely Anglo-American, the American movement is not entirely a revival of British empiricism. To Bacon's knowledge is power, James adds, knowledge is also satisfaction. To Locke's two inlets of knowledge, sensation and reflection, he adds volition. Against Hume's conception of religion as an outworn superstition, an invention of priests, he puts religious experience as an outcome of the passional needs of humanity. James is the brother of the British empiricists; he is likewise their older brother,—older in time and with a wider outlook. As Dickinson Miller has pointed out, they asked—whence it came; he asks—whither it goes; they asked—what were the originals of the conception; he asks—what is to be the effect upon future practical experience.[5]

The massing of contrasts, each viewing James from a different overlook, builds a more three-dimensional portrait of his thought. In his opening Riley contrasts Puritans and deists directly: with James he multiplies the contrasts until they morph into a context.

Whether or not one agrees, it's a superb demonstration of voice melding with vision. But *American Thought*'s structure extends beyond complex sentences and paragraphs crammed with contrasts. It applies to the narrative overall. What starts with Puritanism ends with Pragmatism, what begins with authoritarianism concludes with democracy. The design works wonderfully. The issue is that the mind continues to march on, and it might parade past pragmatism.

In a later edition (1959) Riley adds chapters on "modern realism" and "some French influences," but these must appear as codas, or appendices since the narrative arc remains anchored in pragmatism. In postwar America, however, pragmatism was swamped by continental influences, partly by the intellectual migration of Europeans beginning in the 1930s and partly the rise of analytic philosophy. Woodbridge Riley doesn't get that far, but it's clear that if he wished to, he would have to redesign *American Thought* from scratch. He cannot add ells and retrofit wings indefinitely without the building becoming a shambles. Literature is about art, not just information, and it requires a sense of aesthetic closure.

Detail Through Rhetorical Construction

Clifford Geertz, *After the Fact: Two Countries, Four Decades, One Anthropologist* and *Available Light: Anthropological Reflections on Philosophical Topics*

If Woodbridge Riley expresses the alliance of literature and philosophy (and politics) at the start of the American century, Clifford Geertz aptly demonstrates what it became as that century ended.

Best known for his work in cultural anthropology, Geertz is a sophisticated student of literary styles—in an essay-cum-memoir he notes that he's "tried virtually every other literary genre at one time or another"—and he is the inheritor of cultural traditions upheaved by relativity, uncertainty principles, complementarity, Gödel's paradox, internal narrative told by unreliable narrators, the whole package of modernism, and not least by the recognition that the central concept of cultural anthropology, culture, is virtually impossible to define in any positivistic sense. "We are condemned, it seemed, to working with a logic and a language in which concept, cause, form, and outcome had the same name." In brief, Geertz addresses not only the difficulty of knowing anything but of expressing the difficulty of knowing anything.[6]

So how, in words, does he say what he wants? Here is how he opens his reflection in an essay that serves as an intellectual memoir.

Suppose, having entangled yourself every now and again over four decades or so in the goings-on in two provincial towns, one a Southeast Asian bend in the road, one a North African outpost and passage point, you wished to say something about how those goings-on had changed. You could contrast then and now, before and after, describe what life used to be like, what it has since become. You could write a narrative, a story of how one thing led to another, and those to a third: "and then ... and then." You could invent indexes and describe trends: more individualism, less religiosity, rising welfare, declining morale. You could produce a memoir, look back at the past through the blaze of the present, struggling to re-experience. You could outline stages—Traditional, Modern, Postmodern; Feudalism, Colonialism, Independence—and postulate a goal for it all: the withered state, the iron cage. You could describe the transformation of institutions, structures in motion: the family, the market, the civil service, the school. You could even build a model, conceive a process, propose a theory. You could draw graphs.

There are, in brief, many approaches, each with its disciplinary genre, formulas, and exemplars. An honest assessment, in Geertz's opinion, would admit that nothing in the world is stable, including the disciplines created and the personalities obligated to understand that world.

The problem is that more has changed, and more disjointly, than one at first imagines. The two towns of course have altered, in many ways superficially, in a few profoundly. But so, and likewise, has the anthropologist. So has the discipline within which the anthropologist works, the intellectual setting within which that discipline exists, and the moral basis on which it rests. So have the countries in which the two towns are enclosed and the international world in which the two countries are enclosed. So has just about everyone's sense of what is available from life. It is Heraclitus cubed and worse. When everything changes, from the small and immediate to the vast and abstract—the object of study, the world immediately around it, the student, the world immediately around him, and the wider world around them both—there seems to be no place to stand so as to locate just what has altered and how.

That is the voice of the abstract thinker, assessing the general state of affairs. Now comes Geertz's restatement, in his own terms.

The Heraclitan image is in fact false, or anyway misleading. Time, this sort of time, part personal, part vocational, part political, part (whatever that might mean) philosophical, does not flow like some vast river catching up all its tributaries and heading toward some final sea or cataract, but as larger and smaller streams, twisting and turning and now and then crossing, running together for a while, separating again. Nor does it move in shorter and longer cycles and durations, superimposed one upon another as a complex wave for an harmonic analyst to factor out. It is not history one is faced with, nor biography, but a confusion of histories, a swarm of biographies. There is order in it all of some sort, but it is the order of a squall or a street market: nothing metrical.

And finally, his conclusion:

> It is necessary, then, to be satisfied with swirls, confluxions, and inconstant connections; clouds collecting, clouds dispersing. There is no general story to be told, no synoptic picture to be had. Or if there is, no one, certainly no one wandering into the middle of them like Fabrice at Waterloo, is in a position to construct them, neither at the time nor later. What we can construct, if we keep notes and survive, are hindsight accounts of the connectedness of things that seem to have happened: pieced-together patternings, after the fact.[7]

"After the fact." It's the title of the book that contains the essay, and it conveys the sense that the "facts," however construed, are the elements of existence. There is no universal protocol to render them into "sense," much less objective truth. "It may just be, however, that all understanding (and indeed, if distributive, bottom-up models of the brain are right, consciousness as such) trails life in just this way. Floundering through mere happenings and then concocting accounts of how they hang together is what knowledge and illusion alike consist in. The accounts are concocted out of available notions, cultural equipment ready to hand."

An intellectual life is a life that goes "after the facts" and then finds a way to present them as they are, a method of thick description. "To form my accounts of change, in my towns, my profession, my world, and myself, calls thus not for plotted narrative, measurement, reminiscence, or structural progression, and certainly not for graphs; though these have their uses (as do models and theorizings) in setting frames and defining issues. It calls for showing how particular events and unique occasions, an encounter here, a development there, can be woven together with a variety of facts and a battery of interpretations to produce a sense of how things go, have been going, and are likely to go."[8]

This isn't the stuff of science. It is the stuff of literature, and it is to literature that Geertz turns to express his understanding. The organizing theme is a pun.

Where Woodbridge Riley knew what he wanted to say and was confident that he had the culture behind him, Clifford Geertz is less assertive, sure only that surety is an illusion, confident only that no existing patterns can impose themselves usefully on the experience he wants to describe. So where Riley states baldly and uses classic rhetoric to sharpen contrasts, and G. J. Whitrow is content to rely on the inherited formulas for language and math, Geertz indulges in swirls and word play, uses a subdued rhetoric to layer and bury thoughts in subordinate clauses, and even concocts an informing title out of a pun.

This is prose highly structured rhetorically. It is full of parallelisms, nested qualifying clauses, and hesitations, all of which prevent a thought from bolting freely onward. But note that Geertz does not, similarly, qualify the rhetoric. He compounds it, multiplies it, stretches and shortens it, but he does not surrender it. It might swirl and eddy and locally thicken, amid wordplay piled on wordplay, but it's what holds his arguments about the impossibility of systems together. If anything the rhetoric does to his prose what he claims ideas shouldn't do to data.

However opaque the cultural artifact being examined, the prose is far from mindless, inchoate, or murky. It has a form, though one that permits constant mulling, even self-editing, that does not lead smartly to a foregone conclusion or to a demonstration plot but wends and pokes through thickets and occasionally vanishes in clouds, all of which manages to convey his sense that the only reality ultimately lies in particularities, specifics, the stuff of life, rendered in what he famously called "thick description."

Not surprisingly Geertz wrote no magisterial summas, rather tending to classic novella-length studies from field research and more commonly essays that seem to suit someone committed to the tactile and felt life, with the appreciation that ideas too are the stuff of life; they just need to be centered in particulars, not float transcendently above quotidian existence. What begin as illuminating conceptual contrasts between Indonesia and Morocco blur and dissolve into the only hard nugget possible, the particular.

While Geertz claims that Ludwig Wittgenstein was the inspiration for his interest in the metaphysics of meaning, his oeuvre might best be characterized as Jamesian—William, pluralist and pragmatist, for his thought, and Henry, ever balancing and in his later years convoluted, for his prose. In the end it's not just about thick description but about thickly describing. Whether the viscosity of Geertz's prose assists his ambition or totters on the brink of the imitative fallacy is something individual readers must decide, and will depend on individual taste more than the collective protocols of disciplinary professionals.

Detail Through Dialogue

Steven Squyres, *Roving Mars*: Spirit, Opportunity, *and the Exploration of the Red Planet*

The Mars rovers *Spirit* and *Opportunity* are marvels of engineering, further distilled by the need to both harden and miniaturize. But the same might be said for a book about their creation and deployment. How to describe the invention, manufacture, and operation on another planet of robotic vehicles, while infusing them with the disciplined enthusiasm of a vision quest? How to explain the intricacies of fuses in pyrotechnic cable cutters? The deployment of a parachute on another world with a far thinner atmosphere? The steering of vehicles so distant that radio messages, screaming at the speed of light, take thirteen minutes to reach them? Yet the technology is as critical to the narrative as to the mission. The mission worked because the engineering did. The text will likewise work, or falter, because it can describe why the pieces exist, how they work, and how they got onto the rovers, got to Mars, and then got around Mars. And what is true for the pieces is equally true for the people. A team got the rovers to the Gusev Crater and Meridiani Planum. The book concludes with an appendix of over four thousand names of people who had worked on the project.

As with all exploration literature, the text comes with a built-in narrative arc, which is essentially the hero cycle. The trick here is that the hero is a machine, or more precisely the hero is a team whose alter ego is a robot: *Spirit* and *Opportunity* are literally extensions of their inventors and operators. Translating visions and values into metal and plastic is the core storyline. Transfusing the character of the principal players into those machines is the literary artifice—the textual engineering, as it were.

That the mission comes with deadlines for launch gives tension if not conflict to the plot. The MER—Mars Exploring Rover—team must not only get to Mars, but they must do it on an unyielding timetable. The bulk of the book describes the relentless challenges that emerge and how they are met. Each incident describes a failure and fix, each has its primary protagonist or two, each contributes a tile to the larger narrative mosaic. Each, that is, has a similar literary structure, tweaked to the peculiarities of the problem at hand. What holds the text together is a clear narrative, a quest story, told in Squyres's pragmatic voice—colloquial, direct, vivid, and always on the verge of combustion.

He uses all the stock techniques for conveying tricky information. Here, he uses dialogue:

"What is it?" I asked him.
　　"We screwed up the resistor tests. The current was too low."
　　"We have to do the tests over again?"
　　"Yep."
　　Oh God. "How much were they low by?"

"About an amp."

That didn't sound like much. "What'll happen if we test them at an amp higher?"

"They'll blow," replied Mark. He sounded very sure.[9]

Here, he again uses dialogue to introduce a scene in which he asks someone to explain to him—as a surrogate for the reader—what has happened.

"Hi Steve, it's Pete. We've got a problem."

Oh shit, what now? "What's up?"

"Down at the Cape on Saturday they were doing some chassis isolation impedance measurements of the cruise stage. They expected to see three ohms, and instead they saw 3.8 ohms."

English, Pete. "What's that mean?"

"It means we probably blew the SPG fuse in *Spirit*."

The single point ground fuse was something I knew about. It was actually pretty useless. It had been put into the design to protect touchy hardware against short circuits during ATLO. Bad things can happen when you have a lot of technicians working around a complicated spacecraft. Somebody can drop a screwdriver into powered-up electronics, and bzzzt, you've shorted it out and toasted something. The fuse had been put into the design to protect against that sort of thing. But what the designers who put the fuse in hadn't realized was that the guys who were responsible for the most easily toasted components in the rover were a step ahead of them—they had built in their own protection against shorts. So the fuse wasn't even necessary. But it was in the design now anyway, like it or not.[10]

Here, he relates the story of a parachute test conducted at the mammoth wind tunnel at NASA Ames.

The chute wouldn't open. Instead, it was oscillating wildly in the wind, opening halfway and then closing again, over and over, like a giant sea creature swimming. Slowly Adam realized what he was seeing. He'd never seen it before, but he'd read about it, and he'd heard stories from other parachute designers.

His chute was squidding.

Squidding is a personality disorder of parachutes. Squidding is a monster that waits for parachute designers in the dark. It happens when something's not quite right in the design, when the forces that want to pop the chute open are repeatedly overcome by other forces that flap it closed again. Squidding had never been seen in a parachute like ours before, not in thirty years of testing. But now this chute, the one that Adam was betting would take us to Mars, was squidding.

"Uh . . . we . . ." he said, stammering into his headset, not quite sure what to do, "might as well shut it down." The big fans spun down and the chute started to sag . . . still squidding and then, too late, finally struggling open as the wind subsided.

For five minutes Adam was ill. His wasn't the only crisis on the project, he knew. The airbags were weak. DIMES might not work. Everything was too heavy. But nobody wanted to be the one whose crisis brought the project down, and Adam was no exception. There had to be a fix.[11]

In the end, of course, the team solves the issue. The rovers land safely, and spectacularly, on Mars. There are many such problems, one every few pages, but Steven Squyres, principal investigator, doesn't allow any one to halt the progress forward, and Steven Squyres, author, doesn't allow any one to detour or hijack the narrative, which has its own timeline to satisfy.

Detail Through Discovery

Elizabeth Kolbert, *The Sixth Extinction: An Unnatural History*

The evidence mounts of humanity's maltreatment of the Earth. An unhinged climate, species lost and invasive, a metastasizing population of people, a biosphere rewired for its energy flows and ecologically scrambled, even geochemical cycles of carbon, nitrogen, and sulfur broken and rerouted, all these and more are being summed into the term *Anthropocene*. But the most poignant of all such insults might be what observers are terming the Sixth Extinction. Five times in the past the planet has undergone major upheavals of land, ocean, and climate that resulted in a massive loss of species. A sixth such event seems underway. What makes this one different is that people are the lynchpin.

As the saying goes, a single death is a tragedy, a million a statistic. To make the statistic vivid Kolbert takes a sample of thirteen stories. Each has a common shelf of ingredients—a theme on some aspect of the Anthropocene, a species, a person or group connected to the species, a backstory drawn from history, an explanation drawn from science, and a personal perspective from the author's visits to sites or species. In this way, abstract topics like invasives or ocean acidification become tangible and grounded; they acquire a backstory, a living (or once-living) creature as a kind of mascot, and a human face. Their story can be told by the same techniques used for character profiles. A few species further distill in a single, named individual. The Sumatran rhino (*Dicerorhinus sumatrensis*) gets personified as Suci at the Cincinnati Zoo. The Great Auk (*Pinguinus impennis*) acquires a memorial, if not quite a face, as Count Raben's auk.

The human presence—generic as a cause of the damage, specific as a voice for the species—becomes the moral pith to the book. It is people who have named, studied, used, abused, stumbled over, or in some way driven the species over the brink. Kolbert uses her own presence as a traveler to serve as a docent to create and explain the setting with its particulars of place, people, and creature. Her conversations with researchers create possibility for dramatic dialogue.

This happens thirteen times, but while the parts of the formula repeat, their order does not. The ingredients are stirred and kneaded differently. In effect, the author does with chapters what good writers do with sentences (and paragraphs): she tweaks the structure and varies the tempo. The overall theme remains unchanged: the species before us is extinct or headed toward extinction. But each creature is unique; each history, distinct. The reader senses a familiar pattern without being annoyed by rigid replication.

There are plenty of scientific papers to document the trends and argue the hypotheses about causes. What Elizabeth Kolbert does is translate those ideas into vivid particulars that make the argument without restating her thesis. Take two examples from chapter 10, "The New Pangaea," that deal with the deliberate, and more insidiously, the accidental introduction of species to places without immunity to their ecological infection. Here she illustrates the general theme by retelling the relatively well-known story of the brown tree snake.

The corollary to leaving old antagonists behind is finding new, native organisms to take advantage of. A particularly famous—and ghastly—instance of this comes in the long, skinny form of the brown tree snake, *Boiga irregularis*. The snake is native to Papua New Guinea and northern Australia, and it found its way to Guam in the nineteen-forties, probably in military cargo. The only snake indigenous to the island is a small, sightless creature the size of a worm; thus Guam's fauna was entirely unprepared for *Boiga irregularis* and its voracious feeding habits. The snake ate its way through most of the island's native birds, including the Guam flycatcher, last seen in 1984; the Guam rail, which survives only owing to a captive breeding program; and the Mariana fruit-dove, which is extinct on Guam (through it persists on a couple of other, smaller islands). Before the tree snake arrived, Guam had three native species of mammals, all bats; today only one—the Marianas flying fox—remains, and it is considered highly endangered. Meanwhile, the snake, also a beneficiary of enemy release, was multiplying like crazy; at the peak of what is sometimes called its "irruption," population densities were as high as forty snakes per acre. So thorough has been the devastation wrought by the brown tree snake that it has practically run out of native animals to consume; nowadays it feeds mostly on other interlopers, like the curious skink, a lizard also introduced to Guam from Papua New

Guinea. The author David Quammen cautions that while it is easy to demonize the brown tree snake, the animal is not evil; it's just amoral and in the wrong place. What *Boiga irregularis* has done in Guam, he observes, "is precisely what *Homo sapiens* had done all over the planet: succeeded extravagantly at the expense of other species."[12]

The tree snake that ate Guam is not news. If anything it has become an environmental fable, like the impoverishment of Easter Island. Kolbert retells it here to establish with a well-documented account what can happen in extreme cases. Then she hones in on the particular species highlighted by her chapter, *Myotis lucifugus*, a North American brown bat. What makes the Guam story vivid are the details and the frictionless telling of how the unwelcome snakes gobbled an island. What will make the brown bat story compelling is her personal reaction to being at the site of a mass killing at Aeolus cave in New York.

> "That's what makes this so dramatic—it's breaking the evolutionary chain," Darling said. He and Hicks began picking dead bats off the ground. Those that were too badly decomposed were tossed back; those that were more or less intact were sexed and placed in two-quart plastic bags. I helped out by holding the bag for dead females. Soon it was full and another one was started. When the specimen count hit somewhere around five hundred, Darling decided that it was time to go. Hicks hung back; he'd brought along his enormous camera and said that he wanted to take more pictures. In the hours we had been slipping around in the cave, the carnage had grown even more grotesque; many of the bat carcasses had been crushed, and now there was blood oozing out of them. As I made my way up toward the entrance, Hicks called after me: "Don't step on any dead bats." It took me a moment to realize he was joking.[13]

The carnage becomes personal and real. So does the metaphor that serves as a moral, which has even well-intentioned people blundering around on the carcasses of creatures killed by their unintended actions.

This is a popular imagining of a lot of abstruse concepts and data sets. It's not a textbook, it's not targeted to specialists. It's written for the kind of readership that subscribes to the *New Yorker*. It needs a human interest hook, and finds one by creating scenes with people and by personifying the lost species. It breaks up the white light of a diffuse abstraction like the Anthropocene by refracting it through a prism of personalities.

It's not the only way to explain the Anthropocene, or to carry a message, but it is one of a repertoire of techniques that can broadcast technical information to reach a wider world. Even historians could adapt it by visiting sites, talking to curators and locals, and finding ways to handle stones, artifacts, diaries, and archival documents by attaching them to characters or having them serve a similar literary role.

Detail Through Omitted Transitions

John McPhee, *Encounters with the Archdruid*

Here is a sketch, as background information, on the book's protagonist, David Brower. Normally we would expect to see the known details integrated into a single portrait, as the connective tissue of the text arranges and highlights the particulars. That task, however, can absorb a lot of words and bog down the flow. Sometimes the outcome can be achieved by skipping the conjunctions, the subordinate clauses, and the logical transitioning.

> Brower's father taught mechanical drawing at the University of California. He was a small man (five seven), with a rock-ribbed face and stern habits. His first name was Ross. He never smoked. He did not drink, even coffee. One traumatic day, he came home with the news that he had lost his instructorship. Home was 2232 Haste Street, where the family had two frame houses, one behind the other, that had been partitioned into eleven apartments. For the rest of his life, Brower's father

managed and janitored the apartments. Things became, in Brower's words, "pretty thin," and he remembers holes in his sweaters, holes in his shoes, and paper routes. His father's mother moved in to help with the apartments. She was a high-momentum Baptist who had seen to it that her grandson David was underwater when presented to God. She also saw to it that he always had plenty of housework to do. He washed clothes. She banned card games. She permitted the drinking of hot Jello.[14]

If this was all we knew of Brower, it would also feel "pretty thin." It would feel like a bag of shards, not a mosaic. Not only is it a scatter of facts, but even parallelism breaks down ("holes in his sweaters, holes in his shoes, and paper routes"). But it's backstory, worth a paragraph, not a page. We learn some useful facts about Brower's upbringing, which seem to help explain what he left when he headed to the mountains and why he behaves as he does—interpretations and connections that are left to the reader. If this style were to continue page after page, it would become insufferable. As a change in pace, as a means to inject some facts, it passes.

Detail Through Comparison

Jack Weatherford, *Genghis Khan and the Making of the Modern World*

It would seem odd to announce the significance of your subject through a litany of what it did not do. But that is what Jack Weatherford does in his survey of the Mongol empire.

The Mongols made no technological breakthroughs, founded no new religions, wrote few books or dramas, and gave the world no new crops or methods of agriculture. Their own craftsmen could not weave cloth, cast metal, make pottery, or even bake bread. They manufactured neither porcelain nor pottery, painted no pictures, and built no buildings, yet, as their army conquered culture after culture, they collected and passed all of these skills from one civilization to the next.

This mixture of tangible details packaged in parallelism is effective in good part because it upsets our expectations. We anticipate a catalog of what the Mongols achieved, not what they did not. That celebratory note doesn't come until the last part of a compound sentence that ends the paragraph. In the next paragraph, Weatherford reverses and lists the achievements, again with mounting parallelisms.

The only permanent structures Genghis Khan erected were bridges. Although he spurned the building of castles, forts, cities, or walls, as he moved across the landscape, he probably built more bridges than any ruler in history. He spanned hundreds of streams and rivers in order to make the movement of his armies and goods quicker. The Mongols deliberately opened the world to a new commerce not only in goods, but also in ideas and knowledge. The Mongols brought German miners to China and Chinese doctors to Persia. The transfers ranged from the monumental to the trivial. They spread the use of carpets everywhere they went and transplanted lemons and carrots from Persia to China, as well as noodles, playing cards, and tea from China to the West. They brought a metalworker from Paris to build a fountain in the dry steppes of Mongolia, recruited an English nobleman to serve as interpreter in their army, and took the practice of Chinese fingerprinting to Persia. They financed the building of Christian churches in China, Buddhist temples and stupas in Persia, and Muslim Koranic schools in Russia. The Mongols swept across the globe as conquerors, but also as civilization's unrivaled cultural carriers.[15]

The two paragraphs thus make a nifty tag team. Note how the topic sentence of each paragraph comes at the end, which allows the action to begin immediately. Note, too, the value in using specific examples such as "lemons and carrots" rather than abstract words like *agriculture*, and "noodles, playing cards, and tea" rather than saying *parts of cultures were transferred*. The specifics show the penetration of the exchanges into everyday life (and connect with the everyday life of the reader). And note, especially, the use of bridges not only as a symbol for the mass movement of goods and peoples that was the essence of the empire but as a means to span the two paired passages, one that elaborates on what the Mongols couldn't do and one what they could. It's a good example of classic rhetoric carrying simple words to large effect, and a nice pairing with Gibbon's account of another empire and the language used to describe it.

Interlude

Learning How to Write by Learning How to Read

Reading and writing go together—everyone knows that. But not everyone appreciates how truly interactive the relationship is. Sure, someone has to write a text before we can read it. But almost everyone will learn to read or be read to before he or she learns to write.

We learn to speak by listening; we learn to write by reading. Great writers are voracious readers, and more to the point, they read with an eye to learning craft. Most readers will read a passage, or reread one, because they like what is said, or like how it is said. They agree with its message, or savor the roll of words and the timbre of the voice. In the end, they like it (or not). Most serious writers will reread text that catches their fancy in order to parse it, to disassemble the literary mechanism into its gears and levers so see how, exactly, it moves thoughts into words. They note a particularly skillful use of parallelism; not too strict, suggestive rather than assertive. Or they pause over a passage that lilts with a subtle alliteration. Or they note how an author mischievously tweaks some expected structure to compel a closer reading. Or they marvel at how a dyed-in-the-wool academic might throw his literary voice into the persona of a crusty woodsman. They file those passages according to whatever system suits their style. The repertoire of techniques piles up. Eventually, either by overt imitation or cunning adaptation those lessons will reappear.

Of course you can only learn to write by writing. But that writing will be informed by the reading you've done as it echoes off the pages of your practice.

For some years I've taught a graduate course in nonfiction writing. We begin each session with a discussion of assigned readings, all chosen because they illustrate some literary possibility, and that discussion takes the form of each student identifying two passages that caught their attention and then explaining how they understand that text to work from the perspective of craft. It's equally surprising how many students relish the same passages and how many do not. They are, in effect, mining the assigned texts for techniques. Later smelted into their own voice and taste, the outcome will frequently reappear in the texts they submit for workshopping. Nothing new in this—imitation has forever been the pedagogy of rhetoricians. The students just need to appreciate that their reading will shape their writing, whether consciously or unconsciously, and that it is better to make it conscious.

So in addition to a dictionary and maybe a thesaurus a writer will have a personal anthology of favorite passages for reference. I can think of many. Early on I had imprinted on my literary consciousness a paragraph in Wallace Stegner's biography of John Wesley Powell. What struck me was the graceful way Stegner distilled what could have been a necessary but merely dutiful digest of Powell's upbringing.

It is worth looking for a moment at how he was made.

It is easy enough to summarize: he was made by wandering, by hard labor, by the Bible, by an outdoor life in small towns and on farms, by the optimism and practicality and democracy of the frontier, by the occasional man of learning and the occasional books he met, by country schools and the ill-equipped cubs or worn-out misfits who taught them, by the academies and colleges with their lamentable lacks and their industry and their hope, by the Methodism of his father and the prevailing conviction that success came from work and only to the deserving. If there were not many opportunities, if the cultural darkness was considerable, it was also true that in the darkness any little star showed as plainly as a sun.[1]

Anyone who writes history knows the need to scroll through events or occasionally catalog reasons, factors, influences, and whatnot. What I learned from Stegner is that there is no reason to lamely list them like bullet points. A subtle parallelism—by prepositional phrase rather than whole sentences—disguises the character of the roster, and the if-then structure of the conclusion provides a bit of flourish that aptly sums up what Stegner believes the take-away message is. (John McPhee manages the trick by dropping the transitional scaffolding.)

From time to time I've turned back to that remembered passage and appealed to it to let me reincarnate a laundry list of factors into something more lively. Here's a paragraph from an essay on the evolution of strategies by which to manage the western U.S. fire scene that, like a radio crystal, dimly resonates with that old broadcast.

In retrospect it's easy to see how America's western firescapes evolved into an alloy of the big, the costly, and the feral. How prescribed fire became too complex, too expensive, and too laden with liabilities. How concerns with firefighter safety pushed fire agencies to pull back under extreme conditions and hostile settings. How legacy fuels powered more savage outbreaks. How climate change and exurban sprawl removed the buffers, both historical and geographic, that had granted previous generations room for maneuver. How political gridlock over public lands paralyzed agencies like the Forest Service. How costs argued to go big with escape fires and multiple ignitions. How the only fires and smokes that were allowed were, paradoxically, wildfires for which there is no culpable agent. How, in sum, fire agencies have (if silently) ceded an illusion of control, have surrendered beliefs that they can get ahead of the problem, and have sought, with big-box burnouts and point protection, to turn necessity into opportunity.[2]

This is not how the American fire community talks about prescribed fire. But I had a different take on what was happening on the public lands, and I wanted something that would get attention, so I chose a literary technique not common to this community. It annoyed some readers—that's why different is not usually better. It got circulated and discussed, however, which was my purpose.

It's not a strict imitation, and the final sentence keeps the broad parallelism rather than spinning off a different construction (that required more than a sentence and got its own paragraph), yet it illustrates what I have had many, many occasions to see in classrooms and my own reading—how parallelism can float (or sink). Its origins were learned long ago by reading *Beyond the Hundredth Meridian*.

Whether or not imitation is the sincerest form of flattery, it is a time-honored method of instruction (and self-learning), and the essence of rhetoric as a discipline. I've adapted all of the exemplars above at one time or another.

That said, not every rhetoric technique can apply to every situation. A strategy of explanation by contrast will only work if the subject is suited to systematic comparison, a syllogism can only work if the topic can be parsed into logic, a story can succeed only if explanation is amenable to narrative. Knowing the options, however, makes it easier to match style and subject.

From Wilfred Thesiger's *Arabian Sands* I borrowed the idea that a simple opening sentence might be sufficient. So in *Vestal Fire* I open with the observation, "Before Europe there was fire." The point is that, contrary to most European notions, fire is fundamental to Earth, not simply a tool of humanity; it predates humans, and it will postdate them. The book ends with the complementary observation that "After Europe there will still be fire." From the *Economist's* profile of Thesiger, I found a usable trope for an article on "burning deserts."

The second thing you notice is the eerie similarity to fires everywhere. The flames crackle through stiff grasses, surge up trunks, flash through tangled brush. Airtankers drop red-retardant slurry, helicopters circle like hawks, and crews clad in hard hats and yellow nomex cut, dig, and burn out. Wildfire and backfire collide.

But that resemblance strikes you only after you pass through the unsettling realization that what is burning is the Sonoran Desert. Not the clichéd metaphors of burning sands, flaming sunsets, fiery or furnace-hot deserts, but the real thing: a Sonoran Desert stocked with grasses, ocotillos, ironwood, chollas, and saguaros. The firefight is genuine. The two fires, metaphoric and real, converge.[3]

And from John McPhee's *Oranges* I thought I had a nifty way to throw readers into the strange world of Ghanaian fire. I hedged my bet, though, and gave the litany a topic sentence (omitted here) before plunging onward:

Pastoralists burn to sweep away encroaching brush, cleanse a site of ticks, inhibit snakes, and shock dormant grasses back to life. Their flocks crowd onto the fresh green fodder, more palatable and more nutritious than the unburned stalks. Farmers burn to clean fields of rice and millet stubble, maize stalks, and sugar cane, or, more broadly, the longer-cycle bush fallow of shrubs and trees. . . . Twi calls February *Ogyefuo*, literally meaning "fire farm"; Akwapin calls it *Apamabere*, "time of collecting smoldering stems"; and Ewe names it *Dzove*, which means simple "burn." Farmers in Bawku will ridicule neighbors as "untidy" and slovenly who have not burned before the first rains. Hunters set fires to smoke rats out of holes and both to drive and to draw game.... The scene is visible from space, imaged through satellites by day in infrared and by night in visible light, a vast spangled constellation of fires, like a Milky Way of burning, winding across the Earth's dark matter.[4]

And so it goes for 770 words, the exotic jostling with the mundane, a single thick-description paragraph that tries to hold the raw stuff that the essay must explain. The point is to profile fire in Ghana, not analyze it for fuel loads or sociological categories, so I thought I could jumble the lot together rather than break the many uses of fire down into six or eight categories and describe each. I hoped the reader would be piqued enough to want to know why so much fire in so many variations flourishes on the Gold Coast. I recalled how I was led on by McPhee's account of oranges. I thought I could create something similar with flames. Fire has been described as a model autocatalytic process, a reaction that once sparked keeps propagating. I wanted to recreate that sense in prose.

7

More Than Words Can Say

Short Narration

In which we contemplate how style can add value to texts of shorter lengths.

Their etymology and origin aligns essays with assays, that is, tests, but of a literary rather than scientific sort. But nonfiction can also be stories, and these tend to be categorized as short (essays) and long (books).

We'll look at three short pieces. The first accents the drama of a trek, and through dramatic highlighting of select incidents, the essay's theme. The second interweaves several actual with symbolic travels in ways that suggest allegory. The third uses a story to make an argument.

Story as Saga

Wallace Stegner, "And Nothing Shall Hinder or Stay Them . . . ," *Mormon Country*

Mormon Country is a collection of essays, first published in 1942, that constitutes a literary reconnaissance of a distinctive culture region, what the first settlers called Deseret and what is now known as Utah. The text displays Stegner's signature style, a fusion of dramatic events and personalities, classical rhetoric, and oft-colloquial diction and sensibility. Two essays trace the central story of Mormonism: the relocation and populating of a refuge among the western mountains. The first essay—"Forty Thousand Saints in One Act . . ."—tracks the original hegira of 1846–47. The second, "And Nothing Shall Hinder or Stay Them . . . ," describes the subsequent surge as it becomes institutionalized, climaxing in the tragedy of the Willie and Martin handcart companies.

The essay begins with a description of the people, the purpose, and the means to transport them.

They were British converts from the Black Belt collieries, broad-spoken proselytes from the dying towns of Cornwall and Wales; they were Manxmen and Norwegians and Danes and Swedes. They were the technologically and spiritually unemployed, many of them, the economically-stranded people of Europe's back doors, to whom the Church offered both material and spiritual rejuvenation, a chance to own and cultivate a little farm, an opportunity to start over again—most of all an opportunity to assure themselves Heaven by gathering to the valleys of Zion and Building up the Kingdom. The religious motivation was the more important, but the economic should not be ignored. These were the same sort of people, living in the same sort of circumstances, as those who in 1844 made economic history by creating the Rochdale Co-operative system in Toad Lane. In that one Lancashire town of Rochdale in 1841, according to a Parliamentary report, there were fifteen hundred people existing on forty-five cents a week. It does not take much inducement to leave that kind of living for the hopeful new, and the Mormon missionaries found their richest field of labor among the millhands and miners of England. They had both inducements: another deal for the economically under-privileged, a hope of heaven for the spiritually depressed. Many of the proselytes from those English towns would have waded through fire to reach the sanctuary in the mountains, and some of them almost literally did.[1]

"Money was a problem" since most of the converts were poor, so a system of transportation loans was devised. "It was an efficient system" in which agents escorted converts to Liverpool and then to Salt Lake City. Most men converts walked the routes, with wagons restricted for supplies, women, children, and the sick. In an effort to reduce costs and speed up the process, Brigham Young dropped the heavy wagons and oxen, and had the emigrants "walk . . . pushing or pulling their rationed supplies and limited belongings in wheelbarrows and pushcarts."[2]

Stegner then injects himself into the proposition, making the abstract personal.

I have been over that route, or its modern equivalent, many times, by car, by bus, by streamliner, by thumb. I have driven it in thirty hours and hitch-hiked it in a day and a half from Iowa City to Salt Lake. But I think that if I had been asked to walk it in 1856, on skimpy rations, pulling my duffle and perhaps my family in a handcart, with hostile Indians possible most of the way, it would have tried my faith. Apparently a trial of faith was just what the emigrants wanted. They not only agreed to Brigham's plan; they jumped at it, and not by dozens but by hundreds. They were already, before their ship had left Liverpool, part of that irresistible line of force that Brigham Young had set up, already dedicated to the annealing and unifying dynamics of the great Idea.[3]

That's the first third of the text. The second focuses on a particular individual, Archer Walters, a carpenter from Sheffield, "not because his story is the most exciting but because it is as typical as any that can be found." Archer makes the proselytizing and the trekking concrete. And because of his skills, he found himself in chronic demand for broken handcarts and other needs. "Under the date of June 4 appears an entry in Archer Walters's *Journal* which runs like a leitmotif through the whole record: 'Made coffin for a child dead in camp.' As carpenter, Walters had plenty of those jobs. He became in fact if not in name, coffin-maker to Israel."[4]

His journal chronicles the trials, but Stegner sharpens them with telling details and a rhetorical parallelism.

> And always there were the coffins. June 15: coffin for William Lee, aged 12, and another for Sister Prator's child. June 17: coffin for Job Willing's son. June 21: coffin for Brother Bowers. June 26: coffin for Emma Sheen, aged two and a half. July 2: coffin for Brother Card's daughter. July 26: coffin Brother Henry Walker struck by lightning in the very middle of the train. Buried without coffin because no boards available. Aug. 17: Brother Missel Rossin found dead by the side of the road. Aug. 31: Brother Stoddard died. Sept. 2: Walter Sanderson died. Sept. 8: Brother Nipras died. Sept. 14: Sister Mayer died....
>
> But they walked it. They killed rattlesnakes by the side of the trail, they labored and sweated over the continually broken carts, they bucked wind and rain and diarrhea and the constant deaths, they waded rivers, some of them a dozen times, and they climbed the long hill to South Pass and over it and on across the Green River Valley with the dust blowing over them and the wind already freezing with unseasonable winter. Their rations were cut, and cut again, and the children whimpered with sore feet and hunger. But they walked it. At the end of September they came out of Emigration Canyon with the remnants of their five hundred Saints, the patched remains of their handcarts, the creaking and dry-axled wagons in which the heavy equipment had been hauled. They arrived with tears and thanksgiving after a walk of fourteen hundred miles.[5]

The repetition of death, the repeated walking. The deaths come in staccato declarative sentences, each a finality. The walking continues across run-on sentences that stumble and swell with the trek.

Sadly, Archer Walters "died of dysentery two weeks after he and his family arrived in Salt Lake, but he undoubtedly died satisfied. He did not live to inherit his mountain valley in the flesh, but his immortality is established. His wife and his five children all survived the migration.

His children, among them, had thirty-seven sons and daughters. His descendants now, eighty-six years after he turned pilgrim, number more than five hundred." So Stegner ends part two, and he shuns the expected easy irony in favor of a tally of survivors, which provides a hopeful counterpart to the roster of those who died on the trail.[6]

The last third of the essay tracks two later handcart companies of 1856, those under Brother Willie and Brother Martin, advised by the Church's agents to wait and overwinter in Iowa but determined to push on regardless. "The story of those two caravans of Saints is a story of tragedy second in western history only to the tragedy of the Donner Party. The only thing the Donner Party did that the handcart companies did not was to eat their dead companions. The Mormons, apparently, were better prepared to die. Their hope was fixed on Heaven, not on the golden shore."[7]

The handcarters were late, winter was early. Rescue parties struggled to reach them in time and bring them through to Salt Lake. Of all the details he might have mustered, Stegner, with a novelist's instinct, again reaches for the heart. "On the 26th Echo Canyon, and a child born. Both mother and child lived. The child was wrapped in the sacrificed underwear, the holy garments, of one of the relief party, and was named Echo. If his name meant anything, if there was in his post-natal memories any echo of what his mother must have borne with him over the bitter road, he must have had a haunted life."[8]

The ordeal ends with 145 dead out of a company of 580. The tragedy ended the handcart experiment. Stegner concludes his narrative by paraphrasing Brigham Young, who "preached a sermon in which he told his people that the scattering of those saintly bones by the coyotes meant nothing. They would arise on the Day in a new and shining garment of flesh and be renewed in Heaven along with the Holy City that they never got to see."[9]

That is the text for the believers. For the others—Stegner was not himself Mormon—his essay serves as a historical sermon that explains why the Willie and Martin handcart companies continue to live in spirit, as symbols of Mormon pioneering resolve. This time, irony tints the text. It's tolerated because Stegner is not making the comment directly but refracting through the words of Young, though it's Stegner who has chosen which of Young's words to repeat and who sets the context that determines the pH of the irony.

Story as Allegory

John McPhee, "The Travels of the Rock," *Irons in the Fire*

To the uninitiated Plymouth Rock would seem a simple entity with a simple history. It's a rock, after all. People might interpret it differently over the years, but a large rock can't have changed much since the Pilgrims landed, and its history can't be particularly complicated. Wrong. Instead, John McPhee presents a complex, layered text in which the revered rock both moves and displays a history that eerily echoes that of the United States. The need to repair the rock (the latest rehab) gives a story line that allows the other narratives—the narrative of the rock as stone and the narrative of the rock as symbol—to hold together.

The opening three paragraphs distill the theme, but the opening line itself is surely among the strangest in popular literature: "Plymouth Rock is a glacial erratic at rest in exotic terrane." It's hard to imagine a lead, and in some ways topic, sentence like that running the gauntlet of writing workshops and serial edits. But the rock is first of all a rock. The sentence summarizes its geologic history. McPhee then establishes the way in which the rock will travel through American history and its various imaginations, beginning with earth scientists (and so told with scientific citation).

When Mayflower, an English merchant ship, approached the rock, in 1620, the rock, like the ship, had recently been somewhere else. Heaven knew where. Some geologists have said the rock is Laurentian granite, from north of the St. Lawrence River (Loring, 1920). Most American geologists have preferred a provenance closer to home: Cape Ann, for example, north of Boston (Carnegie Institution, 1923); or the region of Cohasset, south of Boston (Shimer, 1951); or even the bed of Plymouth Bay (Mather, 1952). Wherever the boulder came from, it was many times larger in 1620 than it is today.

It was also in one piece. In 1774, the rock was split in two, horizontally, like a bagel. There were those who feared and those who hoped that the break in the rock portended an irreversible rupture between England and the American colonies. If so, the lower half was the Tory half, for it stayed behind, while the upper part of was moved from the harborside to Liberty Pole Square for the specific purpose of stirring up lust for independence. Scarce was independence half a century old when a new portentous split occurred, in the upper, American, rock. It broke, vertically, into two principal parts, shedding fragments to the side. Eventually, the two halves of the upper part were rejoined by common mortar, containing glacial pebbles from countless sources, and the rock as a whole was reconstructed. The upper part was returned to the waterfront, where a thick filling of mortar was slathered on the lower part, and Plymouth Rock—with its great sutured gash appearing like a surgical scar—was reassembled so that it would be, to whatever extent remained possible, a simulacrum of the landmark that was there in 1620.

In the course of the twentieth century, the mortar did not hold. Pebbles fell out. Chunks. Despite a canopy over the rock (McKim, Mead & White, 1921), water got into the great crack, froze, and wedged against the bonding force with pressures as high as two thousand pounds per square inch. The rock could not stay whole, and on August 7, 1989, in an item disseminated by the Associated Press, the Massachusetts Department of Environmental Management announced that the oldest symbol of the New World was in dire need of a mason.[10]

Archibald MacLeish famously wrote that "a poem should not mean but be." A good poem contains its own meaning in its designed words. So it is with "Travels of the Rock." No explication of its parts can replicate the overall effect. But we need to try or at least give illustrations. The arc is not linear, not a grand narrative except in its significance to American popular culture. It's a composite of tiny tales and vignettes. The history of Plymouth Rock consists of many small stories, some from geologic history, some from American history, some from contemporary times. There is the story of how the parent rock got to Massachusetts; how the rock, as a glacial erratic, got to Plymouth Bay; how the rock was used, moved, and enshrined; how it split, more than once, and eroded; how it was given rods and mortar to hold it in place; how each phase of its travels was deciphered by geologists, historians, locals, and tourists. The rock tells a complex story. The story of how that story acquired meaning runs in parallel and often in counterpoint. The alchemy lies in how McPhee orchestrates them.

Here is the latest version of how the grander terrane came to be.

As plate theorists reconstruct plate motions backward through time, they see landmasses now represented by Europe and Africa closing together with North America during the Paleozoic Era. These were the assembling motions that produced the great continent Pangaea. Much more recently, western Pangaea split apart to form the Atlantic Ocean, which is young, and is widening still. The ocean that was closed out in the making of Pangaea—the older ocean, the ancestral Atlantic, which used to be approximately where the Atlantic is now—is commonly called Iapetus, since Iapetus was the father of Atlas, and plate theorists, in studied humility, thus record their debt to mythology. The collision as [geologist E-an] Zen and others see it in the rock they study and the data they otherwise collect, was not a simple suture of the two great sides. There were islands involved, and island arcs—Madagascars, New Zealands, Sumatras, Japans. "They were large islands in an ocean of unspecified size," he said. "Islands like Newfoundland." Some of them may have amalgamated while still standing off in the ocean. Some not. In one way or another, they were eventually laminated into Pangaea, and slathered like mortar between the huger bodies of rock.

A couple of hundred million years later, as the Atlantic opened, bits and pieces of original America stuck to Europe and rode east. The Outer Hebrides, for example, are said to derive from the northern North American continental core.

HEBRIDES CANADIAN

The converse was true as well. Stuck to North America, fragments of Europe stayed behind. Baltimore, for example. Nova Scotia. A piece of Staten Island.

The part of Massachusetts that includes Plymouth and Boston is now understood to derive from overseas. If from Europe, part of New England could be part of Old England, a New Old England in an Old New England or an Old Old England in a New New England. The May-flower people landed where they left.[11]

Note the use of modern examples—"Madagascar, New Zealand"—sure to be understood by readers to explain the geologic dockings that merged into New England. The wry conclusion is a deft way to complicate the notion of a simple landing—human dockings—as a chronicle of American history.

Here a tale of how the rock—an erratic of American history—moved into national legend:

In November and December of 1620, Mayflower people landed (and slept) in half a dozen places before reaching and settling in Plymouth. In the two contemporary accounts of the Plymouth landings—the several landings of the exploring sloop, and the arrival of the ship itself—nowhere is it mentioned, or obliquely suggested, that anyone set foot on a rock (Mourt, 1622; Bradford, 1630–50). Yet by 1820 the rock was set in the diadem of the republic. Daniel Webster, as the principal speaker on Forefathers' Day, on the two-hundredth anniversary of the Plymouth settlement, said, "Beneath us is the rock on which New England received the feet of the Pilgrims." He continued for an hour, his eloquent images provoking tears, and no one seemed to doubt him. The media had long since accepted the story. "The Federalists toasted their ancestors with the hope that the empire which sprung from their labors be as permanent as the rock of their landing" (*Colombian Sentinel*, December 22, 1798). And when Plymouth's first official history was published it said, "The identical rock, on which the sea-wearied Pilgrims first leaped ... has never been a subject of doubtful designation" (Thacher, 1832). Foreign journalists covering the United States noted in conversations with Americans everywhere what "an object of veneration" the rock had become—a reverence that was growing in inverse proportion to the size of the rock itself. "I saw bits of it carefully preserved in several towns of the Union. . . . Here is a stone which the feet of a few outcasts pressed for an instant, and the stone becomes famous; it is treasured by a great nation; its very dust is shared as a relic" (Tocqueville, 1835).[12]

The rock of course is neither simple nor stable, and any narrative that depends on those properties will falter into legend, an unstated observation aptly conveyed by the patchy, nonlinear presentation. At the same time the allegory is so closely presented—not reasoned so much as laid out—that McPhee does not allow his text to be sucked into quagmires of historiography or politics. The actual histories are so complex they sail beyond casual irony.

McPhee trusts his reader, as the adage goes. Or more particularly he trusts his reader's general knowledge of America's historical experience so the allegory unfolds almost of itself. McPhee provides the information that most people won't know: they complete the fugue by matching that information against their existing lore. The prose is lapidarian, spare, with little slack: it stands like the rock, while tide and tourists wash around. It's a design not unlike the ruptures and mortars and artificial cage that hold and display the rock itself.

He assesses the latest state of the rock through the efforts of Paul Choquette, a mason, to repair it. Choquette comes from South Dakota. The mortar he uses "came from three or four New England states and much of eastern Canada, and, in turn, from almost any Old World country south of Lapland." Plymouth Rock is a mongrelized stone with a history of travel. The society that has enshrined it is a society of immigrants, a fractious country held together by ad hoc repairs among changing circumstances and conflicting interpretations. Choquette notes that "this rock is already eighty per cent gone. Even if we can preserve ten per cent of it, we should preserve it. What matters is what it means."[13]

But what it means to geologists, what it means to historians, what it means to popular culture—all seem to change over time, and yet to converge in ways that make the preservation of what remains of the rock matter. The rock degrades yet persists. The people understand poorly, yet come. McPhee concludes with two visitors, the week before Thanksgiving, a man from Florida and a woman from California, thus triangulating the country. The woman wanted to stop; the man didn't. "It's a rock! Nothing ever happens to it." Yet he finds himself caught up in the drama.[14]

That was my sentiment as well. I didn't care about Plymouth Rock. The Northeast seems boring and contentious. I checked the length of the text before starting, unwilling to invest too much in what, for my reading travels, would be a layover. I was on my way to places elsewhere. Yet, like the Floridian, I found myself caught up in the layered stories. Even rocks can hold compelling narratives, if there is a deft narrator to tell their tales.

Story as Argument

Tom Wolfe, "The Invisible Artist," *Hooking Up*

Now consider an illustration of story as argument. In *The Painted Word*, Tom Wolfe satirized the New York art world as both incestuous and opaque. In "The Invisible Artist" he expands that critique by contrasting the elite art world with a popular challenger.

Frederick Hart died at the age of fifty-five on August 13, 1999, two days after a team of doctors at Johns Hopkins discovered he had lung cancer, abruptly concluding one of the most bizarre stories in the history of twentieth-century art. While still in his twenties Hart consciously, pointedly, aimed for the ultimate in the Western tradition of sculpture, achieved it in a single stroke, then became invisible, and remained as invisible as Ralph Ellison's invisible man, who was invisible "simply because people refused to see me."

Not even Giotto, the twelve-year-old shepherd boy who was out in the meadow with the flock one day circa 1280, using a piece of flint to draw a picture of sheep on the face of a boulder, when the vacationing Florentine artist Cimabue happened to stroll by and discover the baby genius—not even Giotto could match Frederick Hart's storybook rise from obscurity.[15]

In brief strokes Wolfe tells Hart's early life: the child of a broken family, "packed off to an aunt in a part of rural South Carolina where people ate peanuts boiled in salty water"; a juvenile delinquent and high-school dropout; a brief fling at the University of South Carolina, based on an ACT score of 35 (out of 36), until expelled for joining a civil rights protest; a clerk's job at the National Cathedral in Washington, D.C.; a hard-won apprenticeship as a sculptor. In 1971 the cathedral held an international competition for a sculptor to "adorn the building's west facade with a vast and elaborate spread of deep bas-reliefs and statuary on the theme of the Creation." Hart won. "A working-class boy nobody had ever heard of, an apprentice stone carver, had won what would turn out to be the biggest and most prestigious commission for religious sculpture in America in the twentieth century."[16]

"The project brought him unimaginable dividends." He married "a stunningly beautiful" model. He "fell in love with God," became a Roman Catholic, and "began to regard his talent as a charisma, a gift from God." In 1982 he completed the centerpiece of the Creation tableau, *Ex Nihilo*, and waited anxiously for reviews. There were none. No one praised, no one condemned, no one paid any attention. "The truth was, no one did [cared], not in the least. *Ex Nihilo* never got *ex nihilo* simply because the art worldlings refused to see it." Frederick Hart was everything contemporary art disdained: uneducated, overtly religious, uninitiated into the New York scene, given to figures instead of abstractions, a throwback to the Renaissance. "By 1982, no ambitious artist was going to display skill, even if he had it." What Hart did was "nonart." He was ignored.[17]

At this point the story of Frederick Hart's life transforms into an argument, which emerges from Wolfe's chiseling in a way not unlike human forms emerging from blocks of stone. One part of Wolfe's essay is an attempt to place Hart's obscure biography before the literate public. But the other is to use that story as a club with which to beat the "three thousand curators, dealers, collectors, scholars, critics, and artists in New York" who constituted the closed-loop "art world" and who had chosen to ignore Hart's masterpiece.[18]

Hart lurches "from bafflement to shock, then to outrage. He would force the art world to see what great sculpture looked like." This time the conflict hinges on the Vietnam War memorial. Hart entered the competition as the only sculptor to rely on representational figures, specifically three infantrymen, one kneeling beside a fallen comrade while another runs toward them, a kind of martial *Pieta*. The jury selected the ultimate in abstract designs from Maya Lin. "Absolutely skill-proof," as Wolfe puts it. When the Vietnam veterans demanded a statue, Hart got the commission. But again, while Lin's memorial rang brazenly throughout the art world, Hart's *Three Soldiers* was mentioned only in passing. "Why mention the artist, since it's nonart by definition?" The essay then notes other contemporary sculptors who suffered the same fate.[19]

"Over the last fifteen years of his life Hart did something that, in art-world terms, was even more infra dig than *Ex Nihilo* and *Three Soldiers*: he became America's most popular living sculptor." Art-worldlings, in

Wolfe's words, "regarded popularity as skill's live-in slut." So even as Hart devises new techniques, becomes wealthy, assembles a "cadre of like-minded souls, a handful of artists, poets, and philosophers," to "take art back from the Modernists," his work is ignored by the Establishment. Here is American cultural history at its classic finest: popular culture wants one kind of art, elites want another.[20]

The essay ends with a leap from Hart's career to just that larger theme. Might the wheel be turning away from Modernism? If so, "Frederick Hart will not have been the first major artist to have died ten minutes before history absolved him and proved him right." From the standpoint of literary craft the issue is not whether Wolfe's assessment about a reaction to Modernism is right—he wrote the essay in 2000, art criticism is notoriously a matter of taste, and Modernism is still standing. The issue is how he uses a story, in this case a biography, to advance an argument and perhaps a cause. A direct thesis would have bogged down and, given Wolfe's saucy voice, perhaps grated. A story can replace that thesis with a theme. It can absorb Wolfe's raucous voice and its asides and become informative and entertaining whether or not it wholly convinces the reader.[21]

8

More Than Words Can Say

Long Narration

In which style must interweave with scale to enhance aesthetic satisfaction and add thematic value.

It's hard to avoid the conclusion that sometime during the 1970s narrative fell out of favor among professional historians. The reasons are many, some spanning the guild collectively and some as knots of personal taste. There was a desire to become more like a social science and less like a humanities; more a discipline of hard data and hypotheses, and less a text-based scholarship. In America social history swept the field, keen to rewrite the past in ways that would include peoples previously pushed to the margins or off the page, to bring history to the peoples without it. There was an urge to distinguish professional history from journalism, for which "story" was shorthand for sentimental human interest or sensationalism. There were philosophical and literary criticisms, aptly symbolized by Hayden White's *Metahistory*, that made narrative, as narrative, inherently suspect. There was a desire to have academic historians speak to the issues of the day, notably civil rights, and the need to incorporate other peoples and sources of evidence. Since the old narratives had ignored many peoples, narrative itself became tainted as part of the old, maybe oppressive order.

Stories were good, narratives noisome. Stories, often recorded from oral sources, could serve as data, as an alternative to the written texts that had long provide the hard rock of historical evidence. But narratives as devices for synthesizing sources tended to—had to—leave stuff out in order to achieve closure. It was an aesthetic mandate: some arc of coherence had to prevail. If you didn't like that arc, or couldn't find a way to organize the new sources under it, and professional historians in the United States largely didn't and couldn't, it seemed easier to dismiss narrative altogether. William Cronon nicely summarized the quandary in 1992 in his "A Place for Stories," in which he argued that people were a story-telling species, but that narrative with its basis in teleology and its need for closure was a tricky means to find truth. Stories were irrepressible: narrative was inherently suspect. It had to be kept within a larger frame of community taste and judgment.

The concern affected all varieties of narrative. But the special glory of narrative has always been its capacity to absorb large amounts of sources and then arrange them into a thesis or theme that shows development over time, and this is ideally suited to long, syncretic texts such as the books beloved by the humanities. Complex change over time, after all, is practically a working definition of history. Moreover, narrative is more capacious and flexible than many of its academic critics might think. "Arcs" can be made of many smaller arcs; many strands can be woven together to make a braided span; many voices can be orchestrated to fashion a narrative chorus. The aesthetic demand for narrative closure does not, in itself, drive toward a single triumphalist theme. There are brief narratives, working narratives, grand narratives. The nominal failures of narrative are more often failures of literary imagination and skill in their writers.

Narrative is a choice. It doesn't suit every project, purpose, temperament, or taste. But there are ample instances of it used wisely and effectively, and of it judiciously adapted to the particular circumstances of a writer's theme. A few such examples follow.

Classic Narrative

Pierre Berton, *The Klondike Fever: The Life and Death of the Last Great Gold Rush*

The Klondike gold rush can be told many ways—and has been. But its distinctive origins, its geographic locale, the febrile wave that characterizes the stampede and its collapse, all lend themselves to old-style narrative on a grand scale. The subject itself follows an internal arc as it begins with a point of origin, spreads by contagion into a social movement, and then dies off. It's a life cycle, the cycle of a fever, as the book's title suggests. What makes this particular topic ideal, however, is that the events unfold amid an isolated geographic setting. The events concentrate on a place where the action begins and ends, and the stampede must find routes into that place. The historical action thus plays out across a clearly defined geographic setting. The fever segues into a quest. It's a perfect formula for narrative.

A prelude sketches the landscape, a place that predates people and will, by implication, postdate their rush. The first chapter relates the tale of eccentric prospectors and how, by chance, they stumble upon an extraordinarily rich deposit of accessible gold. Then the discovery filters into Dawson and Circle City. The subsequent chapters 3–8 describe, in sequence, how the discovery made its way to the outside world, how "Klondicitis" reached epidemic proportions, how a mass of infected people sought to reach the diggings by the various trails possible, all of them formidable and all of the efforts made concrete by focusing on the recorded memories of actual participants. The race is on; suspense builds; the struggles strew stragglers along the paths. The competition climaxes at Chilkoot Pass, made famous in a photograph, and the flotilla of homemade boats that raft toward the Klondike. Then come two chapters for the primary termini: one on Dawson City as it effervesces into the San Francisco of the North, and one on Skagway as it sinks into the corrupt rule of Soapy Smith. Then, as the gold plays out, the fever breaks, captured in a single chapter. The collapse is more sudden than the infection. The chronicle simply ends.

The chronicle, yes. But not the narrative since that depends on a theme, and the power of the theme, on a sense of moral significance. It's not enough to say what happened; a great narrative derives from an assessment of what it all means. The physical geography that opens the book has a complement in a moral geography to close it. The ending (and its moral judgment) should, in good narrative, suffuse the entire text, and what moves *The Klondike Fever* beyond the realm of adventure story is that Berton's judgment mingles astonishment at the resolve and tenacity of the Klondikers with an appreciation that they left with so little of the material wealth and fame they ostensibly sought.

The richness of the text comes not just from technical proficiency in arranging hundreds of tiles—of quotes, events, personalities, details—into a visually coherent mosaic, but from the tension that so strenuous an undertaking yielded so little wealth and wrought so much damage to those who participated.

The statistics regarding the Klondike stampede are diminishing ones. One hundred thousand persons, it is estimated, actually set out on the trail; some thirty or forty thousand reached Dawson. Only about one half of this number bothered to look for gold, and of these only four thousand found any. Of the four thousand, a few hundred found gold in quantities large enough to call themselves rich. And out of these fortunate men only the merest handful managed to keep their wealth.

The kings of Eldorado toppled from their thrones one by one.[1]

The real payout was in character. "Sprinkled across the continent were thousands of men stamped indelibly with the Klondike experience." An "extraordinary number of public figures" were former Klondikers; so were the "most heavily decorated group of combatants in the Canadian Army." The "Klondike experience had taught all these men that they were capable of a kind of achievement they had never dreamed possible.

It was this, perhaps more than anything else, that set them apart from their fellows"—and what allows Berton to reach beyond casual irony, as it justifies his focus on characters, which collect in the narrative like nuggets in a placer.[2]

A great narrative requires a great storyteller as much as a great story.

Narrative as Serial Mosaic

Peter Hopkirk, *The Great Game: The Struggle for Empire in Central Asia*

The phrase "great game" described the sometimes overt, often covert rivalry between Britain and Russia over Central Asia, with India as the prize. Peter Hopkirk fills in the larger panorama with a historical gallery of stories and anecdotes. Each story seems chosen for its dramatic impact. By concentrating on a single region, a defined span of time, and a conflict between two imperial powers played out on terrain alien to both of them, the narrative has effective boundaries. It's contained in place, time, and action. All in all, what results is a sweeping narrative, though not a comprehensive one. It's a narrative by elision and epiphany because it leaps from event to event as one might hop stones across a river.

The prologue effectively announces the theme and tenor.

On a June morning in 1842, in the Central Asian town of Bokhara, two ragged figures could be seen kneeling in the dust in the great square before the Emir's palace. Their arms were tied tightly behind their backs, and they were in a pitiful condition. Filthy and half-starved, their bodies were covered with sores, their hair, beards and clothes alive with lice. Not far away were two freshly dug graves. Looking on in silence was a small crowd of Bokharans. Normally executions attracted little attention in this remote, and still medieval, caravan town, for under the Emir's vicious and despotic rule they were all too frequent. But this one was different. The two men kneeling in the blazing midday sun at the executioner's feet were British officers.[3]

One of the two, Captain Arthur Conolly, coined the term "Great Game," though it became famous through Rudyard Kipling's use of it in *Kim*.

The episode encapsulates the seriousness of the larger scene, as well as Hopkirk's choice of voice and interests. The text supplies enough background to establish the causes and continuing prods for the Central Asian rivalry between Russia and Britain, but it doesn't bother with all the prescribed food groups of formal scholarship: it makes no pretense to be scholarly, only sufficiently accurate and cohesive to keep the story hopping from incident to incident.

The book has three parts, which unfold as a simple narrative should. "The Beginnings" establishes the origins, "The Middle Years," which ends with Conolly's death (portrayed in the opening), and "The Climactic Years," in which the rivalry reaches its apex before exhaustion leads the deep combatants to resolve their issues with the Anglo-Russian Convention of 1907. Meanwhile the Russian revolution has begun, and both countries will be dragged into a first world war that will exhaust both. The Great Game ends with the Great War.

It's a rattling good yarn, full of adventure and exotic ambience. The book makes no claim to larger significance: it simply aims to grant the Great Game a story of its own beyond the oft-cited phrase. It certainly highlights the way central Asia, including Afghanistan, merits its other sobriquet, the graveyard of empires. In that sense it's a cautionary tale that speaks to contemporary geopolitics. But the book's appeal lies in its relentless tempo.

Considered as craft, the text usefully illustrates how to fashion a strong narrative. How to assemble short tales into a larger one. How to highlight individual characters within a broader tableau. How to keep telling without stopping to tell about. Holding everything together is the sheer energy of the rivalry (and Hopkirk's narrative vigor in the telling), as the Russians seek to advance while the British try to halt them, even if it means a forward strategy that commits the British to advance in return. It's a classic formula for big-screen narrative.

The backstory could be richer, though this is true of most histories. The theme could have a sturdier moral sense beyond courage amid adversity. The text could show flashes of irony, particularly the deep irony of what such adventuring could mean to the larger culture. But as popular history, as an introduction to a region and a rivalry both of which (if as avatars) remain relevant, and as a narrative composition, *The Great Game* works. No book has to be all things to all people. This book does what it sets out to do.

Braided Narrative

George Packer, *The Unwinding: An Inner History of the New America*

The Unwinding tells how America changed from 1978 to 2012. As an "inner history," it refracts the larger trends in politics, economics, and social order through forty-seven separate sketches. Some of the sketches are minibiographies, some are stand-alone essays, some are profiles of places, institutions, and years. There is, in brief, a lot of detail, and a lot of people and experiences assembled. This omnium-gatherum includes both elites and common folk. It's a sample of American society, of course, but a robust one.

The theme is the disaggregation of the American way of life, which fragments in ways that make it difficult for those living through the years to understand what is happening and to bring coherence to their lives both as individuals and as a commonwealth. The forty-seven pieces capture the sense of that disintegration nicely. The problem, of course, is that the text as a whole must not be incoherent. It cannot unwind as it imagines American society doing. It needs organizing devices to give the

pieces a thematic and an aesthetic unity. While the cavalcade of characters, years, institutions, and places is divided into three parts, chrono-
logically broken as 1978–2003, 2004–9, 2010–12. The chosen method to
hold all the pieces together is narrative.

Actually, there are several narratives. One is a chronological unfolding. Events occur in sequence; people age; new stuff builds out of old
stuff. A second is to trace particular topics and especially people as they
experience the era. Three people return in serial fashion as the larger
saga evolves. Dean Price, from North Carolina, represents the economic
changes. Tammy Thomas, an African American in Ohio, telescopes the
social unraveling. Jeff Connaughton, an Alabaman who moves to D.C.,
distills the political rot. Dean's story returns seven times; Jeff's, also
seven; and Tammy's, six. They function as a disaggregated Greek chorus to comment on the changes around them. In addition, there are nine
years (e.g., 1987, 2008) that claim profiles; nine other people, mostly
elites (e.g., Robert Rubin, Sam Walton); and eight places—Silicon Valley (three times), Tampa (four), and Wall Street (one).

All these separate stories need a magnetic-narrative field to hold them
together. That coherence comes from a kind of narrative braiding—less
like a braided rope, mechanically wound, than like a braided stream in
which separate channels converge and diverge as local conditions allow.
It helps, too, that the first person introduced, Dean Price, is also the
last, allowing him to be a cipher for the sum of what has happened. And
of course there is the coherence of voice, bearing a sense of loss and
muted outrage at the metamorphosis of American life. Not least, authorial voice carries the reader across the abrupt transitions between each
of the parts. We don't need explicit segues because we trust the voice,
which in turn trusts us to stay with him.

For those who believe that narrative is worthless unless it conveys
truth, who insist that only hypothesis and evidence can yield positive
information, *The Unwinding* will likely dissatisfy. It portrays an imagined world—one made of real pieces but assembled in a way that pro-
pels the text toward a certain kind of understanding and conclusion.

Not everyone will agree with its premise and its ending; and they will likely attack the means used to reach it. But the real criticism must take the form of a counter-narrative: it must meet this imagined world with another. Both narratives may very well use similar techniques.

Antinarrative: Thesis over Theme

Karl Jacoby, *Shadows at Dawn: A Borderlands Massacre and the Violence of History*

In the early morning of April 30, 1871, a mixed band of O'odhans, Hispanics, and Americans descended on a gathering of Apaches (Nnee) nominally on a reservation and killed 150 men, women, and children. It was one of the worst massacres in American history. But what actually happened? And how might those events be told for today? Karl Jacoby addresses both issues in *Shadows at Dawn*.

The events lend themselves readily to narrative, but each of the participating groups has its own narrative of what happened and why, and each has recorded that day in some kind of formal memory, again in the guise of narrative. No single narrative seems complete. None can trump the others except as political action, the familiar tale of the victors writing history. Underlying the inquiry overall is the question of whether historical scholarship might resolve the relativity of perspectives and meanings—whether it might allow a commentator to stand outside the separate accounts and devise a larger order.

Shadows at Dawn opens with an introduction that lays out issues and tells what the project is about. Then the text attempts to apply those lessons in three parts. "Part One: Violence." Jacoby tells the backstory four times, once for each of the participating groups, each on their own terms. For each this was an act of violence understood in different historical contexts by the O'odhans, the Hispanics (*los vecinos*), Americans, and Nnee. "Part Two: Justice." On the massacre itself the text is silent. Instead, it briefly recounts the trial that followed in which the accused were exonerated on the basis of narrow rulings. "Part Three: Memory." The four groups recount their own memories, which is to say their reflective interpretation, of what happened. And lastly, an epilogue. Here the text ends with an account of a run in relays by Nnee in August 2003 that carried a sacred staff from the outskirts of Tucson to the summit of Mount Graham to protest the construction of an observatory. Meanwhile, the scene of the massacre along Aravaipa Creek is now a nature preserve and wilderness, variously tended by the Nature Conservancy and the Bureau of Land Management. Mount Graham sports a small complex of telescopes. Wilderness and modern science have remade the scenes but in ways that erase cultural presence as a living continuity.

Both transactions challenge not just one memory or another but the value and presence of cultural memory altogether in favor of putatively culture-free landscapes. They are to landscapes what *Shadows at Dawn* is to historiography. Either a multicultural society finds a way to narrate its syncretic history or it abandons the synthetic power of history for ahistorical places, purposes, and disciplines in which no narrative prevails even in an aesthetic sense. The challenge is not just one group's version dominating those of others, but the premise that any of those versions matter beyond clans and tribes. If history is intractable, then scrap history. The future would seem to be one in which meanings that are wholly abstracted beyond any cultural group reign supreme. (With Anthropocenians declaring that we face a no-analogue future the character and lessons of the past may be as irrelevant as traditional means of expressing that past.)

So there seem to be two challenges to narrative, one within the history profession and one between history and the larger culture. *Shadows at Dawn* resolves the first by granting each group its story: it's a kind of narrative pluralism or historiographical agnosticism. All of the participants have their accounts, but the pivotal event itself has no controlling narrative. The past is a "palimpsest of many stories." Instead the text has a thesis to argue that narrative is too imprecise, unstable, and arbitrary to serve the purposes of scholarship. Truth remains in the shadows. The precipitating event is told with silence. In an age of antiheroes, *Shadows at Dawn* proposes an antinarrative.[4]

It says that the obstacles to coherence are too great: it is only by "recounting *all* our stories" and by "listening for the silences between accounts" that we can "capture most fully the human struggle to understand our elusive past." Put this way the historiographical purpose trumps the literary purpose. It says that no grand narrative can orchestrate the smaller narratives. The book's design aligns with this intention, to demonstrate the "fraught relationship between storytelling and historical evaluation." The controversy continues—must continue—and is met with public silence and professional refusal to resolve since the only resolution possible is the appreciation that no unifying narrative is possible. That the book begins with an "introduction" and ends with an "epilogue"—an unsymmetrical pairing since introductions go with conclusions and epilogues with prologues—reinforces the sense that there is no narrative link between start and finish. "Introduction" and "epilogue" are framing devices, not functioning parts of a narrative; the book is a holding pen for small "n" narratives without itself becoming a big "n" narrative. The design thus deftly captures many of the concerns of academic historians in the United States.[5]

This may hold for history as an aspiring positivist science; it is untrue for history as art. There are literary ways to let narrative provide coherence without privileging any single group. The text might have been framed, for example, by a narrative of Karl Jacoby's quest for the meanings of the Camp Grant massacre, or by a story of how the separate narratives become braided or remain separate and so yield the field to ahistorical concepts like wilderness, which aspires to remain untrammeled by the human presence, and science, which claims to seek facts without regard to the ethnicity or historical period of the people making observations. Since, Jacoby argues, narrative is suspect, he cannot use it. Yet while narrative cannot resolve theses, it can express them, and the requirements for aesthetic closure do not bias the thematic outcome.

His argument may satisfy the profession, but by denying that history can provide a common narrative, it implies that history has no national story of how America's many stories can jostle along with some sense of shared purpose. Instead, history becomes the academic voice of each group. It surrenders any claim to larger standing in the society and so yields the field to alternative disciplines and concepts that do not seem bonded to clans, that speak to universal themes (whether true or not), and that hold to a no-analogue future.

The abandonment of history at the massacre site may be a metaphor for the abandonment of history as something to transcend particular tribes. A history of silences can segue into the silence of history. Narrative has its foibles and liabilities. So does the absence of narrative.

Antinarrative: Gloss over Events

Jill Lepore, *The Name of War*

Like scientists who don't use their data to tell stories but tell stories about how they got their data, some contemporary historians tell stories about how the histories of whatever interests them get told. Unreliable narrative yields to historiography, and historiography, for the literary minded, to extended exegesis. The theme becomes the historical search for a theme—or the close textual study of the documentary sources.

In the case of Jill Lepore's *The Name of War* that process does double duty because the book is about people trying to use words to create intellectual borders out of a confused and contested patch of the past generally known as King Philip's War. "This is a study of war, and of how people write about it." People use words to describe war, and they war over those words. King Philip's War serves up a specific example of this general truth. America's endless wars in the Middle East carry the process of war and words into the present.[6]

Instead of narrative anchors, the text relies on frames to hold it together. In this case there are a lot of preliminaries. First is a text titled "What's in a Name?" but which otherwise avoids labels as to its genre, not an author's note, not a preface, not an introduction, that announces the book's thesis. It serves as a kind of extended epigraph, and itself begins with an epigraph. To insert it into the main body of the book could unbalance the larger text, if only by tone. Their styles are slightly askew: one tells, one shows. One bites off less than it chews, the other chews a lot more than it bites off. It's tricky to fuse the two styles. A brief chronology of the major events of the war then follows—necessary because the text follows a topical and literary logic, not a narrative one. The preliminaries conclude with a map.

Still, an artful text needs to begin and end in ways that support the theme. Lepore does this with a prologue and epilogue, the one analyzing a particularly revealing scene from the war, and the other, ways in which the war have been memorialized in stone by later generations. "The Circle" opens with a long quotation from William Hubbard in 1677 on the torture and execution of a prisoner, a Narragansett, held by Mohegans, while around, in a circle, he and other English colonists watch. The episode is a miniature of the war and the difficulties in parsing its meanings. The treatment ends with Lepore noting that "when we read Hubbard's account, we stand in that circle today. We can't help but be drawn into his narrative . . . ," and in repeating it, she seeks to draw in her own readers as well.

There follow four topical explorations of the war and its words—on language, on war, on bondage, and on memory—all based on close reading of original documents, an extended commentary not on events, but on the reports of events and on the ways those events were recorded. This is disquisition, a gloss, which can be contained by scholarly reading, not narrative, which is implicitly regarded as too fraught. The war's many words are, she argues, a search for borders and identities; so her words also need some bounds around them. Like the war, the text has to end. This happens with an epilogue that bookends the prologue.

"The Rock" describes a past written into stone. One sample is the Mount Hope Rock at Bristol, Rhode Island. Who chiseled the inscription? In what language? To what purpose?—all are open to interpretation.

(It may even be a hoax.) The search for an explanation leads Lepore into a discussion of the determination and tenacity of the regional Indian tribes to survive. That quest segues into public commemorative stones, most notably the Great Swamp Monument at South Kingstown, Rhode Island. "In September 1992, some fifty people gathered at the same site, in a circle around those same four boulders and solitary granite shaft. . . ." Lepore is there, personally identifying herself as the teller, so she can again bring us, the readers, into the circle. "To me," Lepore writes, "watching that dance around that circle during a research trip, the scene powerfully echoed" the episode related by William Hubbard's in his 1677 *Narrative*. This time Narragansetts formed the circle. This time, too, narrative control has shifted to the Indians. Historiography, if not history, has come full circle.[7]

The Name of War has a "then" and a "now" and an in-between filled with words about words, organized into theses. The upshot is to so clog any sustained narrative with words that it slows to the point of stalling, of becoming inert, not unlike the granite obelisk at the Great Swamp Monument. Instead, the text becomes about all those words, among them Lepore's, which would seem to argue her point. The Narragansetts may have seized contemporary control over the war's interpretation, but Lepore, by so encircling the event with words, has made a comparable claim regarding the war's future histories. She leaves the readers dancing around the text-as-monument.

Narrative as Dialectic

David Van Reybrouck, *Congo: The Epic History of a People*

Congo is a region, not a truly coherent political entity like a normal country, although a nation has claimed the title and powers of a state. Its people are in reality many peoples who had little say in their gatherings and regatherings, and who share little in common save a collective suffering. "Epic" suggests a grand saga that joins disparate pieces into a unified narrative, and central Africa seems to have no inherent organic principle that exfoliates through time. But while Congo seems an exercise in historical anarchy, *Congo* is an artful mash-up of history, ethnography, biography, and touches of memoir whose coherent narrative is a marvel of literary design.

The organizing principle is a deep dialectic—actually, two dialectics—through time. One plays between individual people and their settings. There are plenty of big movements that tramp through such as imperialism and subsequent decolonization; but the action and its meaning attach to individual people who provide testimonies and serve as touchstones of authenticity. Van Reybrouck acts as a cipher for the Congolese to tell their stories. The other dialectic is between central Africa and Europe. Until Portuguese explorers arrive, the place is a mist of prehistory, lacking form and rhythm. Afterwards, the encounters between newcomers and indigenes set the tempo and tension of the narrative. At times the book reads like a literary fugue, though without a stifling sense of formality; there is little predictable or formulaic about what unfolds.

As much as *Shadows in the Dawn*, *Congo* offers a meditation on the nature of history. The text opens with the Congo River, flowing deep into the Atlantic, still disgorging debris from its past journey through Africa. So it is with time, and the particles of the past that make it into the future. "Where does the history begin?" Van Reybrouck, trained as an archaeologist, wants nontextual data as well as written documents, and he is particularly partial to "living witnesses." This is after all a history of people, not just of a place. Dates matter to Van Reybrouck, though he admits they are "a relative thing in Congo." Incredibly, he finds Nkasi, who claims to have been born in 1882 and knew a boy, Lutunu, who had traveled with Stanley. Incredibly, he finds corroborating evidence, though Nkasi would have to be 126 years old. Van Reybrouck has his point of departure. Suspect dates, lost evidence, conflicting stories— none prevents him from crafting a narrative that manages to hold them coherently into a single text.[8]

There is a strong if muted structural order to *Congo*. The first two chapters orbit around two powerful personalities with different visions of what Congo as a political and economic entity might be. The first introduces Henry Stanley, an archetypal freebooter, though one sanitized by an identity as an explorer; there are others, like Tippo Tibb, a slaver from Zanzibar. The second chapter centers on Leopold II, a political freebooter, as it were, who sets the region on an improbable and largely regrettable path. Chapters 3–6 tell the story of the Belgian Congo after the state had to clean up the wreckage left by Leopold. Chapters 7–14 relate the botched decolonization and its implacable chaos. A final chapter ("www.com") carries the story into contemporary times, in which China begins to replace Europe as an economic influence.

The larger frame is, first, the rise and, finally, the partial eclipse of Europe's presence. Before Europe arrives, the story is inchoate, misty with myth, with only a few broad themes looming like landforms out of the fog. After China enters, the narrative structure again breaks down, partly because the events are too recent for historical parallax and partly because the driving dialectic dissolves. The framing is thin: the long middle narrative is what holds the text together, and the dramatic mortar that bonds it are the biographies and recollections of particular individuals because Congo traces a long trail of failed institutions; what remains are specific persons who have a tale to tell and an author as archaeologist who digs and collects the fragments and assembles them into a collective reconstruction, turning ephemera into witnessed history.

There is plenty of big-screen pageantry, often lurid, which Van Reybrouck summarizes in panoramic paragraphs:

> That Congo, during the first six months of its existence, would have to deal with a serious military mutiny, the massive exodus of those Belgians who had remained behind, an invasion by the Belgian army, a military intervention by the United Nations, logistical support from the Soviet Union, an extremely heated stretch of the Cold War, an unparalleled constitutional crisis, two secessions that covered a third of its territory,

and, to top it all off, the imprisonment, escape, arrest, torture, and murder of its prime minister: no, absolutely no one had seen that coming.

And it would take a long time for things to get better. The period between 1960 and 1965 is known today as the First Republic, but at the time it seemed more like the Last Judgment. The country fell apart, was confronted with a civil war, ethnic pogroms, two coups d'état, three uprisings, and six government leaders (Patrice Lumumba, Joseph Ileo, Justin Bomboko, Cyrille Adoula, Moïse Tshombe, and Évariste Kimba), two—or perhaps even three—of whom were murdered.…[9]

It's hard to find simple themes amid such pandemonium.

The big events get their allotted words, as befits international news, but so do individuals who lived through them, none of whom would have formal, historical identities apart from what Van Reybrouck gives them. It is through them that the abstract events acquire particularized meaning. The book is full of vivid portraits, cameos of common folk, sketches of unrecorded communal life, recovered texts, the felt life of tumultuous times. The famous mingle with the forgotten, but all are genuine Congolese eyes, ears, and voices.

Van Reybrouck manages to ponder how to make a history amid the scatter of suspect sources and the inherited forms of expression without denying those forms or ceding to chaos. He accepts the flaws but rather than discard them seeks to mold them into a more usable medium. Over and again, his informants say how they preferred the flawed order of later colonial times to the lethal disorder that followed. Van Reybrouck seems to have a similar sentiment toward written history.

At times the text seems like Congo itself, ready to burst or dissolve, but it continues, beating to its internal dialectic, adapting literary style to circumstances as the people do their lives, and in the end telling a coherent narrative of an incoherent place and time.

Interlude

Nonfiction as Literature

What makes good nonfiction writing? It has to be honest with its materials, and it has to be readable. The first obligation means you can't make stuff up and you can't leave out stuff that truly affects the argument, theme, or narrative. The second means a reader can understand what you are saying, and it usually means there is some pleasure and extra value in the prose. Even if the subject is less than enthralling, you might keep reading because the writing, the voice, or the texture of the prose is engaging. The design and caliber of the words themselves do work: they convey and add significance. They are not decorative vignettes on the documents, doodled by distracted scribes, but enrich and make the theme more redolent with understanding. What you can't do is pervert the record, the source materials and their relationships, to produce something that contemporary standards of taste deem more pleasing.

That may be the rub. Beyond basic composition, nonfiction writing isn't much taught. It doesn't have expectations, much less standards or canons, that discriminate between robust and feeble prose. It has no aesthetic. Consider, for example, historians. Novitiates are taught historiography, with an emphasis on theses, not on history as texts in which art and craft shape words to advance understanding. Implicit is a choice between emphasizing the writing or emphasizing a theme, but the point of great writing is that you need both. Rhetorical flourish without a point is, well, pointless. And a thesis without art is a seed cast on asphalt.

By contrast, rhetoric, fiction, and journalism are taught, have standard texts, and have a community of like-minded members, most of whom will agree on what—for their times—makes for good and bad writing. Nonfiction outside of journalism doesn't. Instead, someone attracted to, say, literary history—that is, history informed by some sense that the actual writing truly matters, in the same sense that the math underlying a physics theorem matters—will have to look to creative writing or journalism.

Contemporary fiction favors dialogue, or interior thoughts, to express conflict and advance plot. It shifts points of view. It can mingle authorial voice with those of characters. It can destabilize narrative. (Of course there is also genre fiction, in which stock plots are filled with period details.) Journalism has parallel concerns, notably with conversation and character. Dialogue and details—these ground a text and make it vivid. More drama and less description make for better writing. As literary journalism adopts the techniques of fiction, it also absorbs their aesthetic, and the temptation can be strong to tweak the actual facts to "improve" the prose to satisfy that aesthetic.

Yet what can lead nonfiction writers astray may be less an inappropriate craft than a misplaced art. A writer who wants to be recognized as a writer will bend toward the gravitational pull of the strongest aesthetic. That norm is clearly set by fiction, and apart from matters of technique, fiction writers seem to be colonizing realms of nonfiction. The memoir has become the realist novel of today. The personal essay is dissolving into the short story. And of course New Journalism has had a long shelf life. If what is recognized as good writing looks like certain kinds of fiction, then aspiring writers will emulate that style and veer toward fictionalizing.

To continue with history as an example, there are plenty of opportunities to focus on character and conflict, and to find diaries, letters, and transcripts that allow for the sort of dialogue and interior monologues that suit contemporary taste, and to track down telling details from the sources of the time and place; and good historians who also want to be good writers will flock to those possibilities. Most will trend toward narrative.

But history must also cope with such matters as institutions, ideas, traditions, movements of peoples, evolving systems of economics and politics, and for environmental historians, natural processes. Good history, too, must both tell and tell about, narrate and analyze, give the play-by-play and the color commentary within one text. Such difficulties cry out for a literary imagination that can support those tasks without polluting the text. Where is the guidebook of literary devices to show how? where the exemplars? where the art?

The standards for scholarship are fairly clear. The standards for writing are not. The tension between hewing to facts and writing a prose infused with aesthetic appeal can be acute. But creative tension has always been the nuclear core of art. At least some writers of nonfiction will want to be recognized as writers as well as researchers, and there are awards for nonfiction writing, but the standards behind that writing are neither established nor taught. Until they are, the norms of fiction and journalism will fill the void.

9

... and Closings

In which, true to theme, the end completes the beginning, as we return to our opening texts and explore how to close them.

L et's end with closings to the openings with which we started.

Here was the great South Sea, the Pacific Ocean, and they had brought the United States to its shore....

If they were the firstcomers to this shore they were also the lastcomers, and they had been led here by all who had sought the fact in the dream.

On December 7 1805 the Lewis and Clark expedition moved to the Netul River and went up it to the site Lewis had selected. A detachment went down to Tillamook Head on the Pacific beach, to make salt. The others began to cut timber for the winter post, Fort Clatsop.

Most Christian, most exalted, most excellent and powerful Princes, King and Queen of the Spains and of the islands of the sea: Your Highnesses determined to send me to the countries of India, so that I might see what they were like, the land and the peoples, and might seek out and know the nature of everything that is there.

—BERNARD DEVOTO, *THE COURSE OF EMPIRE*[1]

Everything that was to happen had happened and everything that was to be seen had gone. It was now one of those moments when nothing remains but an opening in the sky and a story—may be something of a poem. Anyway, as you possibly remember, there were these lines in front of this story:

And then he thinks he knows
The hills where his life rose.

. . .

These words are now part of the story.

—NORMAN MACLEAN, "USFS 1919: THE RANGER, THE
COOK, AND THE HOLE IN THE SKY"[3]

This was not a solace, nor for that matter a contempt, that Henry understood. The last time I saw him was two months before he fell to the floor of the 14th Street subway station, one night in Los Angeles when the annual meeting of the American Booksellers Association was winding to a close. He had come by the house on his way to a party and we talked him into skipping the party, staying for dinner. What he told me that night was indirect, and involved implicit allusions to other people and other commitments and everything that had happened among us since that summer night in 1966, but it came down to this: he wanted me to know that I could do it without him. That was a third thing Henry told me that I did not believe.

—JOAN DIDION, "AFTER HENRY"[2]

Consider these closings, as themselves, and as bookends to the texts they open. DeVoto's closing completes a national epic, as America reaches a west coast to match its eastern shore. The grand narrative had built subplot by subplot; now it reverses and ends where it began. It had opened in medieval Spain as an amalgam of dreams and deeds, and it closes with American explorers building a post on the Pacific.

Old visions had become an American dream. Maclean's closing completes the transition from adolescent to adult, returning to the words that opened the story, now understood. Didion's closing completes the pivoting of a life moment, told through the refracted profile of a former editor, the transition to adult author. Henry had told her three things, two explicitly about writing, and one, implicit, about being a writer. The first helps nudge the text along; the third, resolves it.

They all bring thematic closure, but they also bring aesthetic and emotional closure. The reader feels satisfied. The ideas introduced, the emotions stirred, the curiosities piqued, the grace of the voice, all must be brought to a conclusion that seems appropriate to the expectations aroused. There should be no reader remorse for having stayed with the text to the end. An opening must pull the reader in. A closing must leave with the experience satisfactorily remembered.

The end may determine the beginning, as Aristotle argued, but most writers seem to write more interesting openings than closings. In his influential book *On Writing Well*, William Zinsser includes a chapter of eleven pages on leads and endings, of which nine pages are leads. Why?

Partly it's a property of endings, which should be reasonable and arise organically from the text. Scale matters. So does genre. A short commentary can play with endings in ways a lengthy biography may not. And partly it's because a surprise closing is harder to write than a surprise opening, and usually involves unexpected phrasing rather than unexpected conclusions. Let's face it: by the time a reader reaches the end, the action and argument and color have already passed. The grabber opening has no real counterpart since, unlike thriller or mystery novels, a surprise ending in nonfiction cannot be conjured up abruptly. Few readers want the thrill of a deus ex machina surprise, or an outcome they had not expected; they want to see how the threads weave together either with narrative or symbol. Besides, in most historical works they already know how the tale turns out. What they want is to enjoy the retelling, perhaps learn some more details, and savor the author's particular take on what it all means.

Still, there are many ways to close. The closest counterpart to the grabber opening may be the one-line joke, or a sudden crystalline image, that is sometimes used to create a final memory. That's better suited for a speech or commentary. In academic papers it often takes the form of an epigram. Yet an abrupt concluding statement can stay in the mind in ways a belabored, syllogistic narrative or flat declaration of opinion or totting up of causes and factors might not. Sometimes the conclusion is fresh because it refutes expectations, and sometimes because the phrasing is unusual or comes from an unlikely quotation or leaps into an uncommon analogy.

Words need bounds—need borders to hold the right ones in and keep the wrong ones out, need a logic to proceed from beginning to end. The ending may involve a tidying up of the text rather than a climax. Often it is part of a structural frame—a postlude to the opening's prelude, an epilogue to its prologue, a death to a birth, a final sum to a found column of figures. It must refer back to and echo, match, or complete the action or argument begun. It is literally a bottom line. Sometimes, in the form of a coda or unpaired aside, it offers a chance for the author to comment and pass some personal judgments on the material in ways that would seem intrusive if stuck brazenly into the main text.

What all closings must do is satisfy the reader's yearning for closure. That may take the form of a thumping QED. Or the drawn curtains that signify the end of a protagonist's life. Or the emotional resolution of a theme. Some endings may offer thematic closure but all must offer aesthetic closure. They must create the felt sense of a text's completion. They offer a point of rest, if only a kind of angle of repose to the scree of words. Whether or not an ending answers a question completely or fixes a solution to a social problem, whether or not it resolves deeper yearnings, it must bring a sense of literary resolution. A reader may want more, may look forward to a sequel, may seek out other writing on the same theme or by the same author, but puts down the text in hand without a sense of being shortchanged or swindled on the premise and promise of the opening. The text has done what it said it would do.

So there is a craft, and an art, and occasionally a drama to the closing, and it is most appealing when, as an organic narrative should, it closes both style and story with flourish and sometimes majesty. A few examples from short-form and long-form texts will show the possibilities.

Essay as Argument

Isaiah Berlin, "From Hope and Fear Set Free"

Isaiah Berlin's essay is an argument, a theme as thesis. He opens by posing a simple question, "Does knowledge always liberate?" After a lengthy historical and logical survey, he concludes that "the proposition is not self-evidently true, if only on empirical grounds. Indeed, it is perhaps one of the least plausible beliefs ever entertained by profound and influential thinkers."[4]

This is not the conclusion most readers would expect. They certainly wouldn't anticipate it from a thinker of Berlin's establishment gravitas, and part of its impact comes from his playing against type, like a Hollywood actor known for being a tough guy suddenly on the side of the angels. Berlin's is a world of lofty intellect announced in an august voice. His are not everyday musings and are not recounted in everyday words. Most readers would anticipate an argument in favor of his thesis—high ideals supported by high intonations. But he decides that the liberal ambition is not substantiated by the examples of history. The elevated tone clashes with expectations; the abrupt ending leaves no room for qualifications and equivocations. In a way that only colleagues versed in his field might appreciate, the closing is a surprise.

The particulars make for a narrow example—the clientele is small. But it is easy to imagine a similar strategy applied to commentaries written for popular audiences.

Essay as Short Narrative

John McPhee, *Encounters with the Archdruid*

John McPhee is a master of grabber openings, but something of a literary klutz in closings. His books and long-form essays are mosaics of set pieces that establish a theme up front, dramatically, then repeat it rather than develop it. The text could end at many points. The closing doesn't often matter to the structure. But in *Encounters* he has written a gem.

The larger book relates three meetings between David Brower, the archdruid of nature preservation, and developers of one sort or another. The third pits Brower and Floyd Dominy, chief of the Bureau of Reclamation, on a raft trip down the Colorado River. The voyage—a good narrative device—begins below the shadow of Glen Canyon Dam. Dominy has enthusiastically boosted the dam, Brower ardently denounced it. The final run takes the party through Lava Rapids, one of the most treacherous on the river.

Each man has his tells. For Brower it's his ubiquitous Sierra cup, into which he puts everything. For Dominy it's a cigar, the time-honored emblem of a wheeler-dealer developer. As they enter the rapids, Brower has his cup hooked to his belt. Dominy withdraws a cigar. The passage through Lava douses everyone equally.

Water welled up like a cushion against the big boulder on the right, and the raft went straight into it, but the pillow of crashing water was so thick that it acted on the raft like a great rubber fender between a wharf and a ship. We slid off the rock and to the left—into the craterscape. The raft bent like a V, flipped open, and shuddered forward. The little outboard—it represented all the choice we had—cavitated, and screamed in the air. Water rose up in tons through the bottom of the raft. It came in from the left, the right, and above. It felt great. It covered us, pounded us, lifted us, and heaved us scudding to the base of the rapid.

For a moment, we sat quietly in the calm, looking back. Then Brower said, "The foot of Lava Falls would be two hundred and twenty-five feet beneath the surface of Lake Dominy."

Dominy said nothing. He just sat there, drawing on a wet, dead cigar. Ten minutes later, however, in the dry and baking Arizona air, he struck a match and lighted the cigar again.[5]

The passage is a cameo of the entire voyage, pitting together two visions, personified by two men, with two very different reactions to the run through Lava. Brower is forced to comment, in words, what the potential loss of building a dam would be. Dominy speaks with gestures. The prevailing climate allows his dowsed cigar to dry and he relights it. Such is the nature of their symbolic confrontations. There is no final resolution. The forces for development, however much they may be momentarily extinguished, will return. McPhee needs to say nothing further. In truth, any gloss would be a distraction. He has spent the book leading to just this conclusion: the gesture is complete. A striking and classy closing.

Grand Narrative

William Manchester, *The Arms of Krupp, 1587–1968*

The Arms of Krupp narrates a long history of Germanic militarism through the prism of a primary armorer, the family Krupp. It opens with a prologue titled "Anvil of the Reich," in which the assassination of the Archduke Ferdinand in 1914, which sparked the Great War, leads also to the sale of his hunting lodge, Blühnbach, to Gustav Krupp, Germany's leading manufacturer of ordnance. Within the panorama of the lodge lies "one of those peaks" beneath which "the legendary twelfth-century Emperor Frederick Barbarossa is said to lie asleep in a cave, ready to spring to Germany's aid whenever the black ravens circling overhead warn him that the sacred soil of the First Reich is in danger."

The sale is "in a way" a "parable of the era. Since the dawn of modern Europe the mysterious, powerful Krupp dynasty had flourished on war and rumors of war. . . . Thus there is a fine analogue in members of the family entering archducal forests, trigger fingers tense, stalking prey. They were, in fact, symbols of the Fatherland's national mood . . . nothing was quite so phenomenal as this habit of matching the Teuton mood of the moment."[6]

So the theme—recurring German militarism—is introduced along with the family that will serve as its cipher. How will the story end? It concludes with an epilogue titled "Silver in an Old Mirror," suggesting that the present is an old reflection of the past. Since the text is a (very long) history, a meditation into the looking glass should move the reader into the past.

> And perhaps, with that strong sense of continuity which distinguishes this extraordinary old family, thoughts sometimes regress, like a movie reel rewound, the film whirring backward, spinning into the past over episodes remembered, over stories told them in their childhood, and deeper ancestral memories. To scenes of Alfried, gaunt and tight-lipped, in the dock at Nuremberg . . . of themselves frisking on the Hügel lawn in the new feldgrau uniforms with Claus and Eckbert . . . of greeting the Führer with a stiff-armed Hitlergruss as he strode briskly across the great hall of the castle . . . of Alfried pledging himself to the newly formed SS. Back farther, to tales of Gustav's wedding to Bertha Krupp, and S.M.'s mustaches that morning, and how the elegant young baron danced and danced . . . of Fritz's ghastly death, of Gargarethe's meekness with her irascible father-in-law, of Fritz in his youth, sobbing bitterly because the Prinz Karl Regiment of the Baden Dragoons had rejected him as a physical weakling . . . of how the manners of Essen's visitors changed in

the wake of the Franco-Prussian War, the old thoughtfulness yielding
to the haughty, strutting Prussian artillery Offizier . . . of spidery Alfred
lying alone in the dark, scribbling of apprehensions lest some future
catastrophe prevent him from avenging his father's failures:
How easily a fire can break out, you know, and a fire would destroy
everything, everything![7]

Then the real closing, an unwinding through time that demonstrates
the persistence of family, of tribal, of national themes.

Back and back, past the Friedrich Krupps and the Anton and Georg
and Wilhelm and Heinrich Krupps—and the Katharinas and Helenes
and Gertruds and Theodoras, the Krupp Valkyrie—back past the early
black-and-white Westphalian cottages into other times, older than the
written record of Essen's original Krupp or even the Dark Ages; back to
the jumbled terror of the Hercynian forest, when the Rhineland was a
Roman outpost, and men believed in monstrous things, and the barbaric Ruhr lay dark under the moon, its oak and bloodbeech tops writh-
ing in the evening wind like a gaggle of ghosts, and the first grim Aryan
savage crouched in his garment of coarse skins, his crude javelin poised,
tense and alert, cloaked by night and fog, ready; waiting; and waiting.[8]

The idea of national character, a cultural essentialism that can persist through centuries, resonates poorly in contemporary thinking, but
rather than baldly invoking such an argument, William Manchester indi-
rectly evokes that persistence by scrolling selectively back through time.
The final image echoes his opening portrait of the Blühnbach lodge,
resting atop an almost mythological Barbarossa ready to spring to life
when called. Through this device, Manchester goes beyond the question
of whether manufacturers like Krupp have been willing enablers of German militarism and identifies that trait as something forged into a very
deep instinct amid a nightmarish darkness.

Whether or not a reader agrees, and the argument can sound off
key given Germany's subsequent pacifism and remarkably placid

unification, the literary trope is effective in making Manchester's moral vision memorable. Someone with an opposing view could use the same technique; one could even imagine a counterargument in which things actually improve. In the end, believability rests not simply on the rhetoric but on the portrait of the family and its setting across more than 800 pages. The trope only distills: it can't by itself convince.

Barbara W. Tuchman, *A Distant Mirror: The Calamitous 14th Century*

In a foreword Barbara Tuchman spells out her attraction to what became the book's themes: "a desire to find out what were the effects on society of the most lethal disaster of recorded history—that is to say, of the Black Death of 1348–50, which killed an estimated one third of the population living between India and Iceland. Given the possibilities of our own time, the reason for my interest is obvious." Upon investigation the plague proved more consequence than cause, but the fourteenth century remained as an eerie, distorted mirror to the present. "If our last decade or two of collapsing assumptions has been a period of unusual discomfort, it is reassuring to know that the human species has lived through worse before."[9]

The narrative needed a "vehicle," however, and Tuchman found a suitable protagonist in Enguerrand de Coucy VII (1340–97), "the last of a great dynasty and 'the most experienced and skillful of all the knights of France.'" The narrative unfolds in a lush, at times leisurely panorama of place, people, and period, culminating in the wastage of the battle of Nicopolis, after which Coucy, "eldest of captives, never before a prisoner nor a loser," dies in captivity. Along with him die the final pretenses of chivalry. Tuchman concludes her foreword with reference to the Arthurian romances in which the Round Table is "shattered from within" and Excalibur "returned to the lake." So the wheel of the world turns.[10]

The narrative tapestry ends twice—not an uncommon outcome in complex texts such as this one. The internal story ceases with the death of its protagonist and the disposition of his will and the dispersion of his possessions. There follows a quick survey in which "the tormented century sank to a close in keeping with its character." The last word is a more abstract essay on the contrasts between the privileged few and the miserable many, and a hint that the tide was about to change. "If the sixty years seemed full of brilliance and adventure to a few at the top, to most they were a succession of wayward dangers; of the three galloping evils, pillage, plague, and taxes; of fierce and tragic conflicts, bizarre fates, capricious money, sorcery, betrayals, insurrections, murder, madness, and the downfall of princes; of dwindling labor for the fields, of cleared land reverting to waste; and always the recurring black shadow of pestilence carrying its message of guilt and sin and the hostility of God." The times were "to grow worse over the next fifty-odd years until at some imperceptible moment, by some mysterious chemistry, energies were refreshed, ideas broke out of the mold of the Middle Ages into new realms, and humanity found itself redirected."[11]

The book could well end here: it has completed its narrative task. The foreword does not mandate that an afterword follow. Yet a sense of hope amid misery is part of the theme. The original allusion to the Arthurian legend notes that, after dissolution, "the effort begins anew. Violent, destructive, greedy, fallible as he may be, man retains his vision of order and resumes his search." To complete that message Tuchman adds an epilogue. Initially, matters only descend further. "In the next fifty years, the forces set in motion during the 14th century played themselves out, some of them in exaggerated form like human failings in old age." Gradually, population stabilizes, senseless political squabbles and endless wars end in treaties by exhaustion, schisms heal over scars, and "the energies of Europe that had once found vent in the crusades were now to find it in voyagers, discoveries, and settlements in the New World." So the torch, once reduced to glowing embers, rekindles and passes to another generation.[12]

But having centered the narrative around the Sire de Coucy, the book cycles back to the family lineage for the final of its nested denouements. By a single stray thread the barony is tied to Henri IV; the "colossus raised by Enguerrand III in the age of the greatest builders since Greece and Rome" decays but stands through subsequent centuries. In 1917, however, the Norns of history cut the threads as the occupying German army wantonly dynamites it into "acres of tumbled stones." So the story ends, not with recovery, but with a redescent into wreckage. "For 700 years the castle had witnessed cycles of human endeavor and failure, order and disorder, greatness and decline. Its ruins remain on the hilltop in Picardy, silent observers as history's wheel turns."[13]

And so it is with Tuchman's text. The scroll that has been unrolled and inscribed upon for over 500 pages quickly rolls up.

Simon Schama, *Citizens*

Since we opened with Simon Schama's *Citizens* as an example of an opening, there is a seemliness in closing with it.

Citizens is a fully realized—defiantly classic—narrative, which means the epilogue must complete what the prologue announces. Instead of the perplexing elephant offering a meditation on forty years of attempted interpretations after the Bastille, there is Simon Schama offering his own thoughts on why the revolution was violent and took the forms it did. Then come a series of reunions. Lucy de La Tour du Pin had become a refugee to America, but then returns to France; she accommodates and makes her peace. Talleyrand returns; so does Lafayette; and they bring closure to the themes they represent. Then, in a final flair of symmetry, the mundane story of Lucy finds its match in the monstrous story of Théroigne de Méricourt, whose revolutionary ardour never calms but becomes more refined and leads her to an asylum at La Salptrière, where she lived naked, was oblivious to all visitors, and was heard to "mutter imprecations against those who had betrayed the Revolution." Here is where ideal untethered to reality ends: her madness was "a logical destination for the compulsions of revolutionary Idealism." Here "revolutionary memory could persist, quite undisturbed by the quotidian mess of the human condition."[14]

The craft serves the art, which serves the theme. There is more than rhetorical symmetry and artisanal prose at work. The horrifying story of Théroigne also serves as a cautionary parable for those who would reduce history to ideal principles, laws, or templates. Their relative abilities to cope with the quotidian mess of life are what differentiate Lucy from Théroigne, and a narrative history from a model. The details of dress and behavior, the mutterings, the confusions of act and intent, must, for Schama, be in the telling, and for that he must appeal to forms to hold them. The proof of his theme lies not in argued evidence so much as the evoked quotidia. The seeming messiness of this gargantuan if not exactly sprawling text is itself the proof of the author's argument.

The structures to hold them in place lie not in science, or historiography, but in literature. In his prologue Schama observes that "it is not in the least fortuitous that the creation of the modern political world coincided precisely with the birth of the modern novel." It is Schama's insight and achievement to adapt the form of the novel to describe the birth of modern politics.[15]

Harder Than It Looks

So how to end? It depends. It depends on your purpose, on your choice of voice and vision, on how you begin—particularly on how you begin—and if you are careful about craft and have a sense of aesthetics, for an argument or a thesis may or may not convince on the basis of the evidence you muster and on the logic you bring to bear, but if it has no aesthetic closure, it will leave the reader unsatisfied. Endings don't just happen. They are made.

Elmore Leonard's novel *Get Shorty* closes with an unresolved search for an ending. Chili Palmer pitches a movie script based on his life as he is living it. The pitch falters because he can improvise his way through daily happenings but not through a text. He concludes, "Fuckin endings, man, they weren't as easy as they looked."[16]

No, they're not.

Writing Exercises

Anyone wanting to improve writing should find plenty of occasions to do so. Routine and thoughtful attention matter more than genre. But some people find specific guidelines or exercises helpful. Below are the ones I would practice if I were starting out again.

1. Practice writing profiles or sketches about someone famous; someone mostly unknown; an idea; an institution; a place; something in the built environment.

2. Rewrite one of your profiles using only quotations or paraphrases.

3. Retell an episode three ways. Vary by point of view, thesis, use of figurative language, and so on.

4. Write a passage with the rhetorical devices in full display. Rewrite it with the scaffolding removed.

5. Write a passage in the third person. Rewrite it in the first person.

6. Take a favorite passage and rewrite it in a similar style on a topic of your choosing.

7. Write a paragraph three ways: with the topic sentence first, with the topic sentence last, and with the topic sentence as the end of the previous paragraph.

8. Write a review of a favorite book with special emphasis on how it uses literary techniques. Write your review first at 1,500 words, then rewrite it at 1,000 words, and finally write it at 600 words.

9. Describe a person, event, or idea in which some technical knowledge—information not likely common to the general reader—is essential to understanding. Write it in the third-person omniscient, then as a blog, then through a profile of a practitioner (using quotes as possible), and finally as a story.

10. Write a text in which figures of speech matter. Try them at different scales—a phrase, a sentence, a paragraph, an essay.

11. Imagine a book or essay that relies on an organizing metaphor or conceit, and write an introduction for the organizing figure.

12. Take a passage of text from your own writing (or something you have found), and rewrite the opening two ways. Write closings to match.

13. Try your hand at humor—comedy, satire, parody, or comic sketch. If you struggle, write a sketch first as a letter to a friend, then tweak it to suit a larger audience.

14. Write about a historical incident. Write it initially in the third person, as for a scholarly article. Then visit the site and write it in the first person, organized around your trip.

15. Write about an event in which some natural process (wind, flood, hurricane, fire, ice storm) figures. Make the process a character in a literary sense, that is, have it function in the text as a character. Animate without anthropomorphizing.

16. Do the same for an idea. Then for an institution.

17. Describe something (a person, event, idea, place, and so on) through comparison and contrast. The comparison may be physical, moral (through behavior), historical, or whatever seems appropriate to the subject.

Notes

Chapter 1. Openings

1. Joan Didion, "After Henry," in *After Henry* (New York: Vintage, 1993), 15.
2. Norman Maclean, "USFS 1919: The Ranger, the Cook, and a Hole in the Sky," in *A River Runs Through It* (Chicago: University of Chicago Press, 1976), 125.
3. Bernard DeVoto, *The Course of Empire* (Boston: Houghton Mifflin, 1952), 3–4.
4. Anthony Lane, "Big Guy," *New Yorker*, May 26, 2014, https://www.newyorker.com/magazine/2014/05/26/big-guy.
5. George Orwell, "Marrakech," in *A Collection of Essays* (New York: Harcourt, 1991), 180.
6. Ibid., 181.
7. Ibid., 181.
8. Ibid., in *A Collection of Essays* (New York: Harcourt, 1991), 148.
9. Ibid., 149, 156.
10. George Orwell, "A Hanging," in *Collected Essays* (Adelaide, Australia: University of Adelaide, 2014). https://ebooks.adelaide.edu.au/o/orwell/george/o79e/complete.html.
11. John McPhee, *Oranges* (New York: Farrar, Straus and Giroux, 1966), 3–6.

12. John McPhee, *Rising from the Plains* (New York: Farrar, Straus and Giroux, 1987), 3–4.
13. V. S. Pritchett, *The Pritchett Century* (New York: Modern Library, 1997), 649.
14. Ibid., 628.
15. "The Last Explorer's Last Journey," *Economist*, July 24, 1997, http://www
.economist.com/node/152619.
16. Wilfred Thesiger, *Arabian Sands* (New York: Dutton, 1959).
17. Barbara Tuchman, *The Guns of August* (New York: Ballantine, 1962), 1–2.
18. Isaiah Berlin, *The Proper Study of Mankind* (New York: Farrar, Straus and Giroux, 1998), 59.
19. Berlin, *Proper Study*, 1.
20. Berlin, "The Concept of Scientific History," *Proper Study*, 17.
21. Simon Schama, *Citizens: A Chronicle of the French Revolution* (New York: Vintage Books, 1989), 6.
22. Ibid., 3, 15.
23. Ibid., 17.

Chapter 2. Resetting the Scene

1. Adams, Henry. *Mont Saint Michel and Chartres* (New York: Penguin, 1986), 7.
2. Ibid., 7.
3. Ibid., 13.
4. Ibid., 12.
5. Wallace Stegner, *Mormon Country* (Lincoln: University of Nebraska Press, 1970), 44–45.
6. Harold Lamb, *Hannibal: One Man Against Rome* (Garden City, N.Y.: Doubleday, 1958), 54–55.
7. G. V. Trevelyan, *A Shortened History of England* (Baltimore: Penguin, 1942), 13, 15.
8. Roger Crowley, *City of Fortune: How Venice Ruled the Seas* (New York: Random House, 2013), 3–4.
9. Richard Hofstadter, *The American Political Tradition* (New York: Vintage, 1948), 206–7.
10. Martha A. Sandweiss, *Passing Strange: A Gilded Age Tale of Love and Deception Across the Color Line* (New York: Penguin, 2009), 2–3.
11. Ibid., 306.
12. Stephen Greenblatt, *The Swerve* (New York: Norton, 2011), 116.
13. Ibid., 118–19.

Chapter 3. Words on Words

1. Mark Forsyth, *The Elements of Eloquence* (London: Icon, 2014), 7–8.
2. Edward Gibbon, *The Decline and Fall of the Roman Empire* (New York: Dell, 1963), 43.
3. Ibid., 30.
4. Ibid., 17.
5. Francis Parkman, "Montcalm and Wolfe," in *France and England in North America, Volume II* (New York: Library of America, 1983), 856.
6. Harold Lamb, *The Crusades: Iron Men and Saints* (Garden City, N.Y.: Doubleday, Doran, 1930), 94, 96.
7. Richard G. Lillard, *Desert Challenge: An Interpretation of Nevada* (New York: Knopf, 1942), 290.
8. Ibid., 291–92.
9. Wallace Stegner, *Beyond the Hundredth Meridian* (New York: Penguin, 1992), 304–5.
10. Ibid. 201.
11. Barbara W. Tuchman, *The Proud Tower: A Portrait of the World Before the War 1890–1914* (New York: Bantam Books, 1967), xiv–xv.
12. Ibid., 463.
13. David McCulloch, *The Path Between the Seas: The Creation of the Panama Canal, 1870–1914* (New York: Simon and Schuster, 1978), 543.
14. Ibid., 554.
15. David Quammen, *Spillover: Animal Infections and the Next Human Pandemic* (New York: Norton, 2013), 442–43.
16. Ibid., 446, 448.

Chapter 4. The Poisonous Passive

1. http://edge.org/conversation/writing-in-the-21st-century [Steven Pinker interview, June 8, 2014]. Subsequently developed in his book *The Sense of Style* (New York: Viking, 2014), e.g., 132–33.
2. Geoffrey K. Pullum, "Fear and Loathing of the English Passive," published online January 22, 2014, at *Science Direct*: DOI http://dx.doi.org/10.1016/j.langcom.2013.08.009; http://www.sciencedirect.com/science/article/pii/S0271530913000980 (May 22, 2014), 1.
3. Ibid., 9–10.
4. Gifford Pinchot, *The Use of the National Forests* (Washington, D.C.: Government Printing Office, 1907), 31.

5. Ibid., 8.

6. Schama, *Citizens*, 404–5.

7. George Orwell, "Politics and the English Language," 176, and "Reflections on Gandhi," 177, in *A Collection of Essays* (New York: Doubleday, 1954).

Interlude. The Imitative Fallacy

1. Mark Twain, *Life on the Mississippi* (New York: Book of the Month Club, 1992), 57.

2. Ibid., 77.

Chapter 5. Make 'Em Laugh, Make 'Em Laugh

1. W. C. Sellar and R. J. Yeatman, *1066 and All That: A Memorable History of England Comprising All the Parts You Can Remember, Including 103 Good Things, 5 Bad Kings and 2 Genuine Dates*. Seventy-fifth anniversary edition reprint, London: Metheun, 1930, 20–21.

2. Dave Barry, *Dave Barry Slept Here: A Sort of History of the United States* (New York: Ballantine, 1989), 136–37.

3. Thomas Cathcart and Daniel Klein, *Plato and a Platypus Walk into a Bar . . . : Understanding Philosophy Through Jokes* (New York: Penguin Books, 2007), 17.

4. Ibid., 79.

5. Richard Feynman, *"Surely You're Joking, Mr. Feynman!"* (New York: Norton, 1997), 144.

6. C. Northcote Parkinson, *Parkinson's Law and Other Studies in Administration* (Cutchogue, N.Y.: Buccaneer Books, 1957), vii.

7. Ibid., 8.

8. Ibid., 60–61.

9. Ibid., 60–61.

10. Andy Bryan, "Back from Yet Another Globetrotting Adventure, Indiana Jones Checks His Mail and Discovers That His Bid for Tenure Has Been Denied," *McSweeney's Internet Tendency*, October 10, 2006, http://www.mcsweeneys.net/articles/back-from-yet-another-globetrotting-adventure-indiana-jones-checks-his-mail-and-discovers-that-his-bid-for-tenure-has-been-denied.

11. Michael Erard, "A Pledge to My Readers," *The Morning News*, February 24, 2010, http://www.themorningnews.org/article/a-pledge-to-my-readers.

12. Umberto Eco, *How to Travel with a Salmon, and Other Essays* (Boston: Harcourt, 1994), 3.

13. Umberto Eco, "How to Travel on American Trains," in *How to Travel with a Salmon, and Other Essays* (Harcourt, 1994), 27–29.

14. Umberto Eco, "How to Write an Introduction," in *How to Travel with a Salmon, and Other Essays* (Harcourt, 1994), 188–89.

15. Ibid., 190–91.

16. Washington Irving, "To the Public," in *Knickerbocker's History of New York* (Boston: IndyPublish.com, 2007).

17. Ibid., 188–89.

18. P. J. O'Rourke, *All the Trouble in the World* (New York: Atlantic Monthly Press, 1994), 105–06.

19. David Brooks, "The Real Romney," *New York Times*, August 27, 2012, http://www.nytimes.com/2012/08/28/opinion/brooks-the-real-romney .html.

20. Tom Wolfe, *The Kingdom of Speech* (New York: Little, Brown, 2016), 32–33.

21. Ibid., 33–35.

22. Ibid., 35.

23. Ibid., 37.

Chapter 6. Deep Details, Thick Descriptions

1. G. J. Whitrow, *The Natural Philosophy of Time*, 2nd ed. (New York: Oxford University Press, 1980), 1.

2. Ibid., 1–2.

3. Woodbridge Riley, *American Thought from Puritanism to Pragmatism and Beyond* (New York: Greenwood, 1969), v.

4. Ibid., 1–2.

5. Ibid., 327.

6. Clifford Geertz, *Available Light: Anthropological Reflections on Philosophical Topics* (Princeton, N.J.: Princeton University Press, 2000), 3, 13.

7. Clifford Geertz, *After the Fact: Two Countries, Four Decades, One Anthropologist* (Cambridge, Mass.: Harvard University Press, 1995), 1–3.

8. Ibid., 3.

9. Steve Squyres, *Roving Mars: Spirit, Opportunity, and the Exploration of the Red Planet* (New York: Hyperion, 2005), 195.

10. Ibid., 179–80.

11. Ibid., 138.

12. Elizabeth Kolbert, *The Sixth Extinction: An Unnatural History* (New York: Picador, 2014), 203–4.

13. Ibid., 210.

14. John McPhee, *Encounters with the Archdruid* (New York: Farrar, Straus and Giroux, 1971), 28–29.

15. Jack Weatherford, *Genghis Khan and the Making of the Modern World* (New York: Broadway Books, 2004), xxii-xxiii.

Interlude. Learning to Write by Learning How to Read

1. Stegner, *Beyond*, 9.

2. Stephen Pyne, "Burning Deserts," in *Smokechasing* (Tucson: University of Arizona Press, 2003), 141.

3. Ibid.

4. Stephen Pyne, "A Land Between," in *Smokechasing* (Tucson: University of Arizona Press, 2003), 72–73.

Chapter 7. More Than Words Can Say: Short Narration

1. Wallace Stegner, *Mormon Country* (Lincoln: University of Nebraska Press, 1970), 72–73.

2. Ibid., 73.

3. Ibid., 74–75.

4. Ibid., 79, 77.

5. Ibid., 78–79.

6. Ibid., 79.

7. Ibid., 80.

8. Ibid., 82.

9. Ibid., 83.

10. John McPhee, *Irons in the Fire* (New York: Farrar, Straus and Giroux, 1998), 187–88.

11. Ibid., 193–94.

12. Ibid., 199–200.

13. Ibid., 198.

14. Ibid., 216.

15. Tom Wolfe, *Hooking Up* (New York: Farrar, Straus and Giroux, 2000), 131.

16. Ibid., 131–32.

17. Ibid., 134.
18. Ibid., 134.
19. Ibid., 135–36.
20. Ibid., 137.
21. Ibid., 139.

Chapter 8. More Than Words Can Say: Long Narration

1. Pierre Berton, *The Klondike Fever: The Life and Death of the Last Great Gold Rush* (New York: MJF Books, 1958), 417.
2. Ibid., 434–35.
3. Peter Hopkirk, *The Great Game: The Struggle for Empire in Central Asia* (New York: Kodansha International, 1992), 1.
4. Karl Jacoby, *Shadows at Dawn: An Apache Massacre and the Violence of History* (New York: Penguin, 2008), 278.
5. Ibid., 278, 7.
6. Jill Lepore, *The Name of War: King Philip's War and the Origins of American Identity* (New York: Vintage Books, 1998), ix.
7. Ibid., 237–38.
8. David Van Reybrouck, *Congo: The Epic History of a People* (New York: HarperCollins, 2014), 7, 9.
9. Ibid., 281.

Chapter 9. . . . and Closings

1. DeVoto, *Course of Empire*, 552–53.
2. Didion, "After Henry," 22.
3. Maclean, "USFS 1919," 246.
4. Berlin, *Proper Study*, 117–18.
5. McPhee, *Encounters*, 244–45.
6. William Manchester, *The Arms of Krupp: The Rise and Fall of the Industrial Dynasty That Armed Germany at War* (New York: Back Bay Books, 2003), 4.
7. Ibid., 843.
8. Ibid., 873.
9. Tuchman, *Distant Mirror*, xiii.
10. Ibid., xiv-xv, 564, xv.
11. Ibid., 578, 581–82.

12. Ibid., xv, 595.
13. Ibid., 597.
14. Schama, *Citizens*, 875.
15. Ibid., 6.
16. Elmore Leonard, *Get Shorty* (New York: William Morrow, 2011), 291.

Index

About the Author

Stephen J. Pyne is a professor at Arizona State University and the author of over thirty books, most recently *Between Two Fires: A Fire History of Contemporary America* and *To the Last Smoke*, a multivolume survey of America's fire regions. He lives in Queen Creek, Arizona, with twenty-two citrus trees, eighteen chickens, and fifteen Tunis sheep.